W9-COG-585

FIFTH EDITION

CSS Pocket Reference

Eric A. Meyer

Beijing · Boston · Farnham · Sebastopol · Tokyo

CSS Pocket Reference

by Eric A. Meyer

Copyright © 2018 O'Reilly Media, Inc. All rights reserved.

Printed in the United States of America.

Published by O'Reilly Media, Inc., 1005 Gravenstein Highway North, Sebastopol, CA 95472.

O'Reilly books may be purchased for educational, business, or sales promotional use. Online editions are also available for most titles (*http://oreilly.com/safari*). For more information, contact our corporate/institutional sales department: 800-998-9938 or *corporate@oreilly.com*.

Editor: Angela Rufino
Production Editor: Colleen Cole
Copyeditor: Molly Ives Brower
Proofreader: Rachel Head
Indexer: WordCo Indexing Services, Inc.
Interior Designer: David Futato
Cover Designer: Karen Montgomery
Illustrator: Rebecca Demarest

May 2001:	First Edition
July 2004:	Second Edition
October 2004:	Third Edition
July 2011:	Fourth Edition
April 2018:	Fifth Edition

Revision History for the Fifth Edition

2018-04-02:   First Release

See *http://oreilly.com/catalog/errata.csp?isbn=9781492033394* for release details.

978-1-492-03339-4

[M]

Table of Contents

Preface

Cascading Style Sheets (CSS) is the World Wide Web Consortium (W3C) standard for the visual presentation of web pages (although it can be used in other settings as well). After a short introduction to the key concepts of CSS, this pocket reference provides an alphabetical reference to all CSS3 selectors, followed by an alphabetical reference to CSS3 properties.

Conventions Used in This Book

The following typographical conventions are used in this book:

Italic
> Used to indicate new terms, URLs, filenames, file extensions, directories, commands and options, and program names. For example, a path in the filesystem will appear as *C:\windows\system*.

<Italic> inside angle brackets
> Shows text that should be replaced with user-supplied values or by values determined by context.

`Constant width`
> Used to show the contents of files, or the output from commands.

There are further conventions relating to value syntax. These are explained at the beginning of Chapter 4.

Using Code Examples

This book is here to help you get your job done. In general, you may use the code in this book in your programs and documentation. You do not need to contact us for permission unless you're reproducing a significant portion of the code. For example, writing a program that uses several chunks of code from this book does not require permission. Selling or distributing a CD-ROM of examples from O'Reilly books does require permission. Answering a question by citing this book and quoting example code does not require permission. Incorporating a significant amount of example code from this book into your product's documentation does require permission.

We appreciate, but do not require, attribution. An attribution usually includes the title, author, publisher, and ISBN. For example: "*CSS Pocket Reference*, 5th Edition, by Eric A. Meyer (O'Reilly). Copyright 2018 O'Reilly Media, Inc., 978-1-492-03339-4."

If you feel your use of code examples falls outside fair use or the permission given above, feel free to contact us at *permissions@oreilly.com*.

O'Reilly Safari

 *Safari* (formerly Safari Books Online) is a membership-based training and reference platform for enterprise, government, educators, and individuals.

Members have access to thousands of books, training videos, Learning Paths, interactive tutorials, and curated playlists from over 250 publishers, including O'Reilly Media, Harvard Business Review, Prentice Hall Professional, Addison-Wesley Professional, Microsoft Press, Sams, Que, Peachpit Press, Adobe, Focal Press, Cisco Press, John Wiley & Sons, Syngress, Morgan Kaufmann, IBM Redbooks, Packt, Adobe Press, FT Press, Apress, Manning, New Riders, McGraw-Hill, Jones & Bartlett, and Course Technology, among others.

For more information, please visit *http://oreilly.com/safari*.

How to Contact Us

Visit Eric A. Meyer's website at *http://meyerweb.com/* or follow @meyerweb (*http://twitter.com/#!/meyerweb*) on Twitter.

Please address comments and questions concerning this book to the publisher:

> O'Reilly Media, Inc.
> 1005 Gravenstein Highway North
> Sebastopol, CA 95472
> 800-998-9938 (in the United States or Canada)
> 707-829-0515 (international or local)
> 707-829-0104 (fax)

We have a web page for this book, where we list errata, examples, and any additional information. You can access this page at *http://bit.ly/css-pocket-ref-5e*.

To comment or ask technical questions about this book, send email to *bookquestions@oreilly.com*.

For more information about our books, courses, conferences, and news, see our website at *http://www.oreilly.com*.

Find us on Facebook: *http://facebook.com/oreilly*

Follow us on Twitter: *http://twitter.com/oreillymedia*

Watch us on YouTube: *http://www.youtube.com/oreillymedia*

CHAPTER 1

Basic Concepts

Adding Styles to HTML

Styles can be applied to documents in three distinct ways, as discussed in the following sections.

Inline Styles

In HTML, style information can be specified for an individual element via the `style` attribute. The value of a `style` attribute is a *declaration block* (see the section "Rule Structure" on page 5) without the curly braces:

```
<p style="color: red; background: yellow;">Look out!
This text is alarmingly presented!</p>
```

Note that as of this writing, only the content of a single declaration block can be used as a `style` attribute value. For example, it is not possible to place hover styles (using `:hover`) in a `style` attribute, nor can `@import` be used in this context.

Although typical XML document languages (such as SVG) support the `style` attribute, it is unlikely that *all* XML languages will support a similar capability. Because of this—and especially because it encourages poor authoring practices—authors are discouraged from using the `style` attribute, and thus inline styles.

Embedded Stylesheets

A stylesheet can be embedded within an HTML document using the `style` element:

```
<html><head><title>Stylin'!</title>
<style type="text/css">
h1 {color: purple;}
p {font-size: smaller; color: gray;}
</style>
</head>
    ...
</html>
```

XML-based languages may or may not provide an equivalent capability; always check the document type definition (DTD) to be certain.

While `style` elements are often found inside the `head` element, as shown in the preceding example, this is not required. Sometimes stylesheets are embedded near the end of a document for performance reasons.

External Stylesheets

Styles can be stored in a separate file. The primary advantage to using a separate file is that when commonly used styles are collected in a single file, all pages using those styles can be updated by editing a single stylesheet. A downside is that it's generally more efficient to embed all styles (and scripts) into an HTML document in order to reduce network calls, although this downside will disappear as HTTP/2 usage increases.

An external stylesheet can be referenced in one of three ways.

@import directive

One or more `@import` directives can be placed at the beginning of any stylesheet. For HTML documents, this is done within an embedded stylesheet:

```
<head><title>My Document</title>
<style type="text/css">
```

```
@import url(site.css);
@import url(navbar.css);
@import url(footer.css) screen and (min-width: 960px);
body {background: yellow;}
</style>
</head>
```

Note that @import directives can appear at the top (and, according to the specification, *only* at the top) of any stylesheet. Thus, one stylesheet could import another, which in turn would import a third.

link element

In HTML documents, the link element can be used to associate a stylesheet with a document. Multiple link elements are permitted. The media attribute can be used to restrict a stylesheet to one or more media environments:

```
<head>
<title>A Document</title>
<link rel="stylesheet" type="text/css" href="basic.css"
  media="all">
<link rel="stylesheet" type="text/css" href="web.css"
  media="screen and (max-width: 960px)">
<link rel="stylesheet" type="text/css" href="paper.css"
  media="print and (color-depth: 2)">
</head>
```

It is also possible to link to alternate stylesheets, but few browsers provide a way for users to make use of them. As of this writing, most or all known user agents load all linked stylesheets, including the alternate stylesheets, regardless of whether the user ever needs them.

xml-stylesheet processing instruction

In XML documents (such as XHTML documents sent with a MIME type of text/xml, application/xml, or application/xhtml+xml), an xml-stylesheet processing instruction can be used to associate a stylesheet with a document. Any xml-stylesheet processing instructions must be placed in the prolog of an XML document. Multiple xml-stylesheet processing instructions are permitted. The media pseudo-attribute can be used to restrict a stylesheet to one or more forms of media:

```
<?xml-stylesheet type="text/css" href="basic.css"
  media="all"?>
<?xml-stylesheet type="text/css" href="web.css"
  media="screen"?>
<?xml-stylesheet type="text/css" href="paper.css"
  media="print"?>
```

HTTP Link headers

The last (and least common by far) way of associating an external stylesheet with your pages is to use an HTTP Link header. This approach uses HTTP headers to replicate the effects of a link element or @import directive.

Adding a line such as this to the *.htaccess* file at the root level of your server will make this happen for all pages on the site, where /style.css is the server path of the stylesheet to be loaded:

```
Header add Link
  "</style.css>;rel=stylesheet;type=text/css;media=all"
```

As an alternative to using *.htaccess*, which has been known to cause performance problems, you can edit your *httpd.conf* file to do the same thing:

```
<Directory /usr/local/username/httpdocs>
Header add Link
  "</style.css>;rel=stylesheet;type=text/css;media=all"
</Directory>
```

where /usr/local/username/httpdocs is replaced with the Unix pathname of your website's actual home directory, and /style.css is replaced with the location of the stylesheet within that home directory.

As of this writing, HTTP headers were not supported by all user agents, most notably Internet Explorer and Safari. Thus, this technique is usually limited to production environments based on other user agents, and the occasional Easter egg for Firefox and Opera users.

Rule Structure

A stylesheet consists of one or more *rules* that describe how page elements should be presented. Every rule has two fundamental parts: the *selector* and the *declaration block*. Figure 1-1 illustrates the structure of a rule.

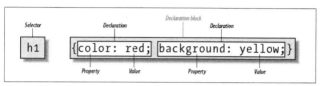

Figure 1-1. Rule structure

On the left side of the rule, we find the selector, which selects the parts of the document to which the rule should be applied. Selectors can stand singly or be grouped as a comma-separated list; e.g., to select the top three heading levels at once, the selector group would be h1, h2, h3. On the right side of the rule, we have the declaration block. A declaration block is made up of one or more *declarations*; each declaration is a combination of a CSS *property* and a *value* of that property.

The declaration block is always enclosed in curly braces. A declaration block can contain several declarations; each declaration must be terminated with a semicolon (;). The exception is the final declaration in a declaration block, for which the semicolon is optional (though recommended).

Each property, which represents a particular stylistic parameter, is separated from its value by a colon (:). Property names in CSS are not case-sensitive. Legal values for a property are defined by the property description. Chapter 4 provides details on acceptable values for CSS properties.

At-rules

A CSS *at-rule* is a statement or block of rules that begins with a specific identifier preceded by an @ sign. These are:

@charset

> Allows an author to define the encoding of the styles within the stylesheet (e.g., @charset "utf-8";). This enables authors to define the encoding of their styles even when they do not control the encoding of the file or system in which the styles are written. If multiple @charset rules are declared, only the first will be used. This *must* be the first line of a stylesheet in which it appears, and *cannot* be preceded by any character. @charset cannot be used in a stylesheet embedded in a document.

@import

> Allows an author to include the styles of another stylesheet (see "@import directive" on page 2). Multiple @import rules are permitted. Any @import rules *must* appear before all other parts of the stylesheet except for @charset.

@namespace

> Allows an author to define an XML namespace to be used in selectors (e.g., @namespace svg url(http://www.w3.org/2000/svg);, permitting the use of svg|a {color: black;} to select <a> elements within SVG files differently than <a> elements in HTML). Multiple @namespace rules are permitted. Any @namespace *must* appear before all other parts of the stylesheet except for @charset and @import rules.

Besides these statements, there are a number of conditional at-rules. These include:

@counter-style

> Defines symbol and counting patterns used in CSS counters (e.g., the numbering of list items in an ordered list).

`@font-face`

Defines an external font to be downloaded and used, including definitions of the identifiers to be used in other style rules. This is part of what is often called "web fonts" or "custom fonts."

`@keyframes`

Defines the states of various steps in an animation sequence, grouped together under a unique identifier.

`@media`

Defines the media types and parameters in which a block of styles are to be applied: e.g., writing `@media (max-width: 600px)` and then the styles to be used for smaller screens. This is the key to Responsive Web Design.

`@supports`

Defines the browser-support conditions under which a block of styles should be used: e.g., writing `@supports (display: grid)` and then the styles that should be used in a CSS Grid–supporting browser.

There are other proposed at-rules which are, as of early 2018, at various stages of development. These include `@document`, `@font-feature-values`, `@page`, and `@viewport`.

Comments

Including comments in CSS is simple. You open with `/*` and end with `*/`, like this:

```
/* This is a comment! */
```

Comments can be multiple lines long:

```
/* This is a comment!
  This is a continuation of the comment.
 And so is this. */
```

They can also occur anywhere within a stylesheet except in the middle of a property name or value:

```
h1/* heading-level-1 */ {color /* foreground color */:
    rgba(23,58,89,0.42) /* RGB + opacity */;}
```

HTML (properly SGML) comments `<!-- such as this -->`
are permitted in stylesheets so as to hide the styles from browsers so old that they don't understand HTML 3.2. They do *not*
act as CSS comments; that is, anything contained in an HTML
comment will be seen and interpreted by the CSS parser.

Style Precedence

A single HTML document can import and link to multiple
external stylesheets, contain one or more embedded stylesheets, and make use of inline styles. In the process, it is quite
possible that some rules will conflict with one another. Cascading Style Sheets uses a mechanism called the *cascade* to resolve
any such conflicts and arrive at a final set of styles to be applied
to the document. Two key components of the cascade are specificity and inheritance.

Specificity Calculations

Specificity describes the weight of a selector and any declarations associated with it. Table 1-1 shows how much each part of
a selector contributes to the total specificity of that selector.

Table 1-1. Selector type specificity

Selector type	Example	Specificity
Universal selector	`*`	0,0,0,0
Combinator	`+`	
Element identifier	`div`	0,0,0,1
Pseudo-element identifier	`::first-line`	
Class identifier	`.warning`	0,0,1,0
Pseudo-class identifier	`:hover`	
Attribute identifier	`[type="checkbox"]`	
ID identifier	`#content`	0,1,0,0
Inline `style` attribute	`style="color: red;"`	1,0,0,0

Specificity values are cumulative; thus, a selector containing two element identifiers and a class identifier (e.g., `div.aside p`) has a specificity of 0,0,1,2. Specificity values are sorted from right to left; thus, a selector containing 11 element identifiers (0,0,0,11) has a lower specificity than a selector containing just a single class identifier (0,0,1,0).

The `!important` directive gives a declaration more weight than nonimportant declarations. The declaration retains the specificity of its selectors and is used only in comparison with other important declarations.

Inheritance

The elements in a document form a treelike hierarchy, with the root element at the top and the rest of the document structure spreading out below it (which makes it look more like a tree root system, really). In an HTML document, the `html` element is at the top of the tree, with the `head` and `body` elements descending from it. The rest of the document structure descends from those elements. In such a structure, elements lower down in the tree are descendants of the ancestors, which are higher in the tree.

CSS uses the document tree for the mechanism of *inheritance*, in which a style applied to an element is inherited by its descendants. For example, if the `body` element is set to have a `color` of `red`, that value propagates down the document tree to the elements that descend from the `body` element. Inheritance is interrupted only by a conflicting style rule that applies directly to an element. Inherited values have no specificity at all (which is *not* the same as having zero specificity).

Note that some properties are not inherited. A property will always define whether it is inherited. Some examples of non-inherited properties are `padding`, `border`, `margin`, and `background`.

The Cascade

The cascade is how CSS resolves conflicts between styles; in other words, it is the mechanism by which a user agent decides, for example, what color to make an element when two different rules apply to it and each one tries to set a different color. Here's how the cascade works:

1. Find all rules with a selector that matches a given element.

2. Sort all declarations applying to the given element by *explicit weight*. Those rules that are marked `!important` have a higher explicit weight than those that are not.

3. Sort all declarations applying to the given element by *origin*. There are three basic origins: author, reader, and user agent. Under normal circumstances, the author's styles win out over the reader's styles. Howerver, `!important` reader styles are stronger than any other styles, including `!important` author styles. Both author and reader styles override the user agent's default styles.

4. Sort all declarations applying to the given element by *specificity*. Those elements with a higher specificity have more weight than those with lower specificity.

5. Sort all declarations applying to the given element by *order*. The later a declaration appears in the stylesheet or document, the more weight it is given. Declarations that appear in an imported stylesheet are considered to come before all declarations within the stylesheet that imports them.

Any presentational hints that come from non-CSS sources (e.g., the preference dialog within a browser) are given the same weight as the user agent's default styles (see step 2 above).

Element Classification

Broadly speaking, CSS groups elements into two types: *non-replaced* and *replaced*. Although the types may seem rather abstract, there actually are some profound differences in how the two types of elements are presented. These differences are explored in detail in Chapter 7 of *CSS: The Definitive Guide*, 4th Edition (O'Reilly).

Nonreplaced Elements

The majority of HTML elements are *nonreplaced elements*, which means their content is presented by the user agent inside a box generated by the element itself. For example, `<span>hi there</span>` is a nonreplaced element, and the text `hi there` will be displayed by the user agent. Paragraphs, headings, table cells, lists, and almost everything else in HTML are nonreplaced elements.

Replaced Elements

In contrast, *replaced elements* are those whose content is replaced by something not directly represented by document content. The most familiar HTML example is the `img` element, which is replaced by an image file external to the document itself. In fact, `img` itself has no actual content, as we can see by considering a simple example:

```
<img src="howdy.gif" alt="Hi">
```

There is no content contained in the element—only an element name and attributes. Only by replacing the element's lack of content with content found through other means (in this case, loading an external image specified by the `src` attribute) can the element have any presentation at all. Another example is the `input` element, which may be replaced with a radio button, checkbox, or text input box, depending on its type. Replaced elements also generate boxes in their display.

Element Display Roles

In addition to being replaced or not, there are two basic types of element display roles in CSS: *block-level* and *inline-level*. All

CSS `display` values fall into one of these two categories. It can be important to know which general role a box falls into, since some properties only apply to one type or the other.

Block-Level

Block-level boxes are those where the element box (by default) fills its parent element's content area width and cannot have other elements to its sides. In other words, block-level elements generate "breaks" before and after the element box. The most familiar block elements from HTML are p and `div`. Replaced elements can be block-level elements but usually are not.

List items are a special case of block-level elements. In addition to behaving in a manner consistent with other block elements, they generate a marker—typically a bullet for unordered lists or a number for ordered lists—which is "attached" to the element box. Except for the presence of this marker, list items are identical to other block elements.

As of early 2018, the `display` values that create block boxes are `block`, `list-item`, `table`, `table-row-group`, `table-header-group`, `table-footer-group`, `table-column-group`, `table-row`, `table-column`, `table-cell`, `table-caption`, `flex`, and `grid`.

Inline-Level

Inline-level boxes are those where an element box is generated within a line of text and does not break up the flow of that line. Perhaps the best-known inline element is the a element in HTML. Other examples are span and em. These elements do not generate a break before or after themselves, so they can appear within the content of another element without disrupting its display.

Note that although the CSS block and inline elements have a great deal in common with HTML block- and inline-level elements, there is an important difference. In HTML, block-level elements cannot descend from inline-level elements, whereas

---

in CSS, there is no restriction on how display roles can be nested within each other.

The display values that create inline boxes are: inline, inline-block, inline-table, and ruby. As of this writing, it was not explicitly defined that the various Ruby-related values (e.g., ruby-text) also generate inline boxes, but this seems the most likely outcome.

Basic Visual Layout

CSS defines algorithms for laying out any element in a document. These algorithms form the underpinnings of visual presentation in CSS. There are two primary kinds of layout, each with very different behaviors: *block-level* and *inline-level* layout.

Block-Level Layout

A block-level box in CSS generates a rectangular box called the *element box*, which describes the amount of space occupied by an element. Figure 1-2 shows the components of an element box.

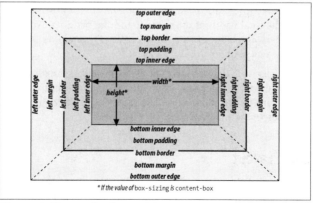

Figure 1-2. The complete box model

The following rules apply to an element box:

- By default, the background of the element box extends to the outer edge of the border, thus filling the content, padding, and border areas (though this can be changed with `background-clip`). If the border has any transparent portions (e.g., it is dotted or dashed), the element background will be visible in those portions. The background does not extend into the margin areas of the box. Any outlines are drawn in the margin area and do not affect layout.

- Only the margins, `height`, and `width` of an element box may be set to `auto`.

- Only margins can be given negative values.

- The padding and border widths of the element box default to `0` (zero), and the border style defaults to `none`.

- If `box-sizing` is `content-box` (the default value), the property `width` defines only the width of the content area; any padding, borders, or margins are added to it. The same is true for `height` with respect to the height.

- If `box-sizing` is `padding-box`, the property `width` defines the total width of the content and the padding. Any borders and margins are added to it. The same is true for `height` with respect to the height.

- If `box-sizing` is `border-box`, the property `width` defines the total width of the content, padding, and borders; any margins are added to it. The same is true for `height` with respect to the height.

Inline Layout

An inline-level box in CSS generates one or more rectangular boxes called *inline boxes*. The following rules apply to inline boxes:

- `width` and `height` do not apply to nonreplaced inline boxes.

- For the properties `left`, `right`, `top`, `bottom`, `margin-left`, `margin-right`, `margin-top`, and `margin-bottom`, any value of auto is converted to 0 (zero).

- For replaced inline boxes, the following rules apply:

  — If `height` and `width` are both `auto` and the element has an intrinsic width (e.g., an image), the value of `width` is equal to the element's intrinsic width. The same holds true for `height`.

  — If `height` and `width` are both `auto` and the element does not have an intrinsic width but does have an intrinsic height and layout ratio, then `width` is set to be the intrinsic height times the ratio.

  — If `height` and `width` are both `auto` and the element does not have an intrinsic height but does have an intrinsic width and layout ratio, then `height` is set to be the intrinsic width divided by the ratio.

There are a few rules even more obscure than those last two; see the CSS box model documentation (*http://w3.org/TR/css3-box/#inline-replaced*) for details.

All inline elements have a `line-height`, which has a great deal to do with how the elements are displayed. The height of a line of text is determined by taking the following factors into account:

Anonymous text

Any string of characters not contained within an inline element. Thus, in the markup:

```
<p>I'm <em>so</em> happy!</p>
```

the sequences "I'm " and " happy!" are anonymous text. Note that the spaces are part of the anonymous text, as a space is a character like any other.

Em-box

The space taken up by a capital letter M in the given font; otherwise known as the character box. Actual glyphs can be taller or shorter than their em-boxes, as discussed in Chapter 5 of *CSS: The Definitive Guide*, 4th Edition. In CSS, the value of `font-size` determines the height of each em-box.

Content area

In nonreplaced elements, this can be the box described by the em-boxes of every character in the element, strung together, or else the box described by the character glyphs in the element. In CSS2.1 and later, user agents can choose either. This text uses the em-box definition for simplicity's sake. In replaced elements, the content area is the intrinsic height of the element plus any margins, borders, or padding.

Leading

The difference between the values of `font-size` and `line-height`. Half this difference is applied to the top and half to the bottom of the content area. These additions to the content area are called, not surprisingly, *half-leading*. Leading is applied only to nonreplaced elements.

Inline box

The box described by the addition of the leading to the content area. For nonreplaced elements, the height of the inline box of an element will be equal to the value for `line-height`. For replaced elements, the height of the inline box of an element will be equal to the content area, as leading is not applied to replaced elements.

Line box

The shortest box that bounds the highest and lowest points of the inline boxes that are found in the line. In other words, the top edge of the line box will be placed along the top of the highest inline box top, and the bottom of the line box is placed along the bottom of the lowest inline box bottom. (See Figure 1-3.

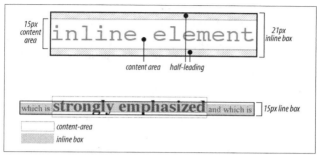

Figure 1-3. Inline layout details

Floating

Floating allows an element to be placed to the left or right of its containing block (which is the nearest block-level ancestor element), with following content flowing around the element. Any floated element automatically generates a block box, regardless of what type of box it would generate if not floated. A floated element is placed according to the following rules:

- The left (or right) outer edge of a floated element may not be to the left (or right) of the inner edge of its containing block.

- The left (or right) outer edge of a floated element must be to the right (or left) of the right (left) outer edge of a left-floating (or right-floating) element that occurs earlier in the document's source, unless the top of the latter element is below the bottom of the former.

- The right outer edge of a left-floating element may not be to the right of the left outer edge of any right-floating element to its right. The left outer edge of a right-floating element may not be to the left of the right outer edge of any left-floating element to its left.

- A floating element's top may not be higher than the inner top of its containing block.

- A floating element's top may not be higher than the top of any earlier floating or block-level element.

- A floating element's top may not be higher than the top of any line box with content that precedes the floating element.

- A left (or right) floating element that has another floating element to its left (right) may not have its right (left) outer edge to the right (left) of its containing block's right (left) edge.

- A floating element must be placed as high as possible.

- A left-floating element must be put as far to the left as possible, and a right-floating element as far to the right as possible. A higher position is preferred to one that is farther to the right or left.

Positioning

When elements are positioned, a number of special rules come into play. These rules govern not only the containing block of the element, but also how it is laid out within that element.

Types of Positioning

There are five types of positioning:

Static

> The element's box is generated as normal. Block-level elements generate a rectangular box that is part of the document's flow, and inline-level boxes generate one or more line boxes that flow within their parent element.

Relative

> The element's box is offset by some distance. Its containing block can be considered to be the area that the element

would occupy if it were not positioned. The element retains the shape it would have had were it not positioned, and the space that the element would otherwise have occupied in the normal flow is preserved.

Absolute

The element's box is completely removed from the flow of the document and positioned with respect to its containing block, which may be another element in the document or the initial containing block (described in the next section). Whatever space the element might have occupied in the normal document flow is closed up, as though the element did not exist. The positioned element generates a block box, regardless of the type of box it would generate if it were in the normal flow.

Sticky

The element's box stays in the normal flow until it reaches a sticky edge of the containing box, at which time it "sticks" there as if absolutely positioned. The space that the element would otherwise have occupied in the normal flow is preserved.

Fixed

The element's box behaves as though set to `absolute`, but its containing block is the viewport itself.

The Containing Block

The containing block of a positioned element is determined as follows:

1. The containing block of the *root element* (also called the *initial containing block*) is established by the user agent. In HTML, the root element is the `html` element, although some browsers may use `body`.

2. For nonroot elements, if an element's `position` value is `relative` or `static`, its containing block is formed by the content edge of the nearest block-level, table-, cell-, or

inline-block ancestor box. Despite this rule, relatively positioned elements are still simply offset (not positioned with respect to the containing block described here) and statically positioned elements do not move from their place in the normal flow.

3. For nonroot elements that have a `position` value of `absolute`, the containing block is set to the nearest ancestor (of any kind) that has a `position` value other than `static`, a `filter` value other than `none`, or a `transform` value other than `none`. This happens as follows:

   a. If the ancestor is block-level, the containing block is that element's outer padding edge; in other words, it is the area bounded by the element's border.

   b. If the ancestor is inline-level, the containing block is set to the content edge of the ancestor. In left-to-right languages, the top and left of the containing block are the top and left content edges of the first box in the ancestor, and the bottom and right edges are the bottom and right content edges of the last box. In right-to-left languages, the right edge of the containing block corresponds to the right content edge of the first box, and the left is taken from the last box. The top and bottom are the same.

   c. If there are no ancestors as described in 3a and 3b, the absolutely positioned element's containing block is defined to be the initial containing block.

Flexible Box Layout

Flexible box layout (also known as *flexbox* or *flex layout*) is ideal for almost any one-dimensional layout; that is, situations where a number of elements need to be placed and distributed along a line. There are two kinds of flex elements: the *flex container* and the *flex items* that are placed within the container.

All the direct children of the flex container element are flex items.

There are two kinds of flex containers: block flexboxes (display: flex) and inline flexboxes (display: inline-flex). These are very much like block and inline-block boxes.

Flex items are laid out in a single line by default, even if this causes the flex items to overflow the flex container. This behavior can be changed using the flex-wrap property.

Figure 1-4 shows the values (and their effects) of the justify-content and align-items properties.

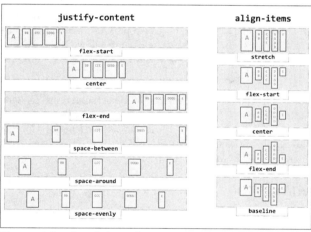

Figure 1-4. Justify and align values

The process of calculating flex sizes is fairly complex. Here's a simplified version of the algorithm:

1. Add together all the hypothetical outer main sizes of the flex items in a flex container. If the sum is smaller than the container size, the *flex factor* is to grow; otherwise, the flex factor is to shrink.

2. Any items that are inflexible are frozen in size. These are:

- Any item with a flex factor of zero
- Any item whose *hypothetical main size* is greater (if growing) or smaller (if shrinking) than its *base size*
- Any item with a growth factor (if growing) or shrink factor (if shrinking) of zero

3. Calculate the *initial free space* by finding the difference between the outer sizes of all flex items and the size of the flex container.

4. Distribute the available free space to the flex items. The amount given to each flex item is initially determined by the ratio of its flex factor to the sum of all the items' flex factors. If an item will be grown past its maximum allowed size, or shrunk below its minimum allowed size, set the size to be the allowed maximum (if growing) or minimum (if shrinking).

Again, this is a simplified version of the actual flex sizing algorithm given in the W3C documentation (*https:// www.w3.org/TR/css-flexbox-1/#resolve-flexible-lengths*). Consult section 9.7 of the CSS Flexible Box Layout Module Level 1 for full details if you want to know more.

Grid Layout

Grid layout is ideal for almost any two-dimensional layout. There are two kinds of grid elements: the *grid container* and the *grid items* that are placed within the container. All the direct children of the grid container element are grid items.

There are two kinds of grid containers: block grids (display: grid) and inline grids (display: inline-grid). These are very much like block and inline-block boxes.

A grid is made up of the following components, as illustrated in Figure 1-5:

- A *grid line* is a horizontal or vertical dividing line within the grid container. These are placed as the author directs and create grid *cells*, *areas*, and *tracks* by implication. Grid lines can be labeled with *identifier tokens*; that's the basis of grid item placement.

- A *grid cell* is any space bounded by four grid lines, with no other grid lines running through it, analogous to a table cell. This is the smallest unit of area in grid layout. Grid cells cannot be directly addressed with CSS grid properties; that is, no property allows you to say a grid item should be associated with a given cell. (But see the next point for more details.)

- A *grid area* is any rectangular area bounded by four grid lines and made up of one or more grid cells. An area can be as small as a single cell or as large as all the cells in the grid. Grid areas are directly addressable by CSS grid properties, which allow you to define the areas and then associate grid items with them.

- A *grid track* is a continuous run between two adjacent grid lines—in other words, a *grid column* or a *grid row*. It goes from one edge of the grid container to the other. The size of a grid track is dependent on the placement of the grid lines that define it. Grid columns and rows are broadly analogous to table columns and rows. More generically, they can be referred to as *block axis* and *inline axis* tracks, where (in Western languages) column tracks are on the block axis and row tracks are on the inline axis.

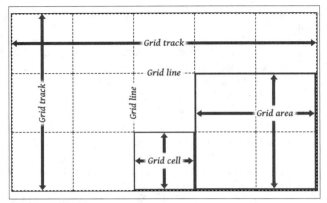

Figure 1-5. Grid layout components

The placement of grid lines can be quite complex, and is accomplished by defining grid track sizes. Between each grid track, a grid line is placed. These lines can be labeled with grid-line names, or left unlabeled and later addressed using numbers.

The formal syntax for defining grid track sizes is quite complicated, but the components are relatively simple to list and explain:

<length> | *<percentage>*
Any non-negative length or percentage value. Thus, 5em defines a 5-em gap between grid lines, whereas 5% creates a gap between lines that is 5% of the total grid length in the given direction (i.e., the horizontal length for grid rows, and the vertical length for columns).

<flex>
A positive real number with the unit identifier fr (e.g., 2fr or 3.14fr) which defines a *flex factor* for the grid track.

min-content
Sets the grid track's width (or height) to be as small as possible while still containing all the content within the grid

track. For example, column tracks that contain only text
will become as narrow as the widest run of text that cannot be line-broken within the track.

max-content

Sets the grid track's width (or height) to be large enough to
contain the largest rendering of all the content within the
grid track. For example, column tracks that contain only
text will become as wide as the longest run of text, *without*
any line-wrapping of the text.

auto

In most cases, auto is equivalent to the largest minimum
size of the grid items occupying the grid track; that is,
once all the minimum sizes of the grid items in the track
have been determined, the track is made as wide as the
widest of those minimums. When auto is used as a maximum value (see minmax() later in this list), it is identical to
max-content.

minmax(*<min>,<max>*)

Sets a range of sizes outside which the grid track cannot
grow or shrink. Either *<min>* or *<max>* can be a *<length>*
or *<percentage>* value, min-content, or max-content.
<max> can be a *<flex>* value, but *<min>* cannot. If the
minimum value computes to be larger than the maximum
computed value, the maximum sizing is ignored and the
minimum size is used as a minimum.

fit-content([*<length>* | *<percentage>*])

Equivalent to minmax(auto,max-content) with an exception: if the track's size is larger than the auto value's computed value, that size can't go higher than the given value
(a *<length>* or *<percentage>*). This is intended to let
authors declare a maximum track size while still letting
the track size be content-bound below that maximum.

repeat([*<integer>* | auto-fill | auto-fit] , *<track-list>*)

Allows authors to repeat a pattern of grid track sizes as
many times as they like. The *<integer>* value must be posi-

tive. `auto-fill` and `auto-fit` delegate the number of tracks to the user agent. *<track-list>* can be any valid combination of track sizes.

There are three kinds of track sizing. These are:

Fixed
> Tracks are given a size in absolute lengths (such as `px` or `em`), or sized with `%`. Percentage values count as fixed track sizes because they are always the same for a given grid container size. The tracks' sizing does not depend on their contents.

Flexible
> Tracks are given a flex or fractional sizing via the `fr` unit. Their sizing does not depend on their contents.

Intrinsic
> The tracks' size is dependent on the things found within them; i.e., with `min-content`, `max-content`, `fit-content()`, and `auto`. These tracks may always be the same size for a given container size and set of content, but they are not regarded as fixed for layout purposes because their contents directly affect their sizing.

The process of actually determining the size of grid tracks, including what to do when track sizes are overconstrained or could lead to circular dependencies, is too long to go into here. In broad strokes, this is the process to find the track sizes:

1. Initialize track sizes, including determining the minimum and maximum sizes for each track. Resolve fixed track sizes to absolute length values. Set intrinsically sized tracks' minimum size to zero and maximum size to unlimited. Flexible tracks are left flexible, with an initial minimum size of zero.

2. Determine the size of intrinsic (e.g., `auto`) tracks, resolving each to an absolute length. First find sizes based on the items within the track, and then gradually add space to encompass items that span multiple tracks.

3. Maximize tracks up to their growth limit (this is determined automatically).

4. Expand flexible (fr) tracks by adding space according to the ratio of each track's flex factor to the total of all flex factors in the grid track.

5. Expand any auto-sized tracks by dividing the remaining free space (if any) by the number of auto tracks and expanding them equally.

The details of each step are quite lengthy, and can be found in section 11 of the CSS Grid Layout Module Level 1 documentation (*https://www.w3.org/TR/css-grid-1/#layout-algorithm*).

Table Layout

The layout of tables can get quite complicated, especially because CSS defines two different ways to calculate table and cell widths, as well as two ways to handle the borders of tables and elements internal to the table. Figure 1-6 illustrates the components of a table.

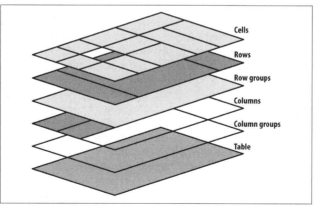

Figure 1-6. Table layout components

Table Arrangement Rules

In general, a table is laid out according to the following principles:

- Each row box encompasses a single row of grid cells. All of the row boxes in a table fill the table from top to bottom in the order they occur in the source document. Thus, the table contains as many grid rows as there are row elements.

- A row group's box encompasses the same grid cells as the row boxes that it contains.

- A column box encompasses one or more columns of grid cells. Column boxes are placed next to each other in the order in which they occur. The first column box is on the left for left-to-right languages and on the right for right-to-left languages.

- A column group's box encompasses the same grid cells as the column boxes that it contains.

- Although cells may span several rows or columns, CSS does not define how that happens. It is instead left to the document language to define spanning. Each spanned cell is a rectangular box one or more grid cells wide and high. The top row of this rectangle is in the row that is parent to the cell. The cell's rectangle must be as far to the left as possible in left-to-right languages, but it may not overlap any other cell box. It must also be to the right of all cells in the same row that appear earlier in the source document in a left-to-right language. In right-to-left languages, a spanned cell must be as far to the right as possible without overlapping other cells, and must be to the left of all cells in the same row that come after it in the document source.

- A cell's box cannot extend beyond the last row box of a table or row group. If the table structure causes this condition, the cell must be shortened until it fits within the table or row group that encloses it.

Fixed Table Layout

The fixed-layout model is fast because its layout doesn't depend on the contents of table cells; it's driven by the width values of the table, columns, and cells within the first row of the table. The fixed-layout model uses the following steps:

1. Any column element whose width property has a value other than auto sets the width for that column.

2. If a column has an auto width, but the cell in the first row of the table within that column has a width other than auto, that cell sets the width for that column. If the cell spans multiple columns, the width is divided equally among the columns.

3. Any columns that are still auto-sized are sized so that their widths are as equal as possible.

At that point, the width of the table is set to be either the value of width for the table or the sum of the column widths, whichever is greater. If the table turns out to be wider than the column widths, the difference is divided by the number of columns and added to each of them.

Automatic Table Layout

The automatic-layout model, although not as fast as the fixed-layout model, is likely to be much more familiar to authors, because it's substantially the same model that HTML tables have used for years. In most current user agents, use of this model will be triggered by a table with a width of auto, regardless of the value of table-layout—although this is not assured.

Here's how the model works:

1. For each cell in a column, calculate both the minimum and maximum cell width.

2. Determine the minimum width required to display the content. In determining the minimum content width, the content can flow to any number of lines, but it may not stick out of the cell's box. If the cell's width value is larger than the minimum possible width, the minimum cell width is set to that value. If the cell's width value is auto, the minimum cell width is set to the minimum content width.

3. For the maximum width, determine the width required to display the content without any line-breaking, other than that forced by explicit line-breaking (e.g., due to the <br> element). That value is the maximum cell width.

4. For each column, calculate both the minimum and maximum column width:

    a. The column's minimum width is determined by the largest minimum cell width of the cells within the column. If the column has been given an explicit width value that is larger than any of the minimum cell widths within the column, the minimum column width is set to the value of width.

    b. For the maximum width, take the largest maximum cell width of the cells within the column. If the column has an explicit width value larger than any of the maximum cell widths within the column, the maximum column width is set to the value of width. These two behaviors recreate the traditional HTML table behavior of forcibly expanding any column to be as wide as its widest cell.

5. In cases where a cell spans more than one column, the sum of the minimum column widths must be equal to the minimum cell width for the spanning cell. Similarly, the

sum of the maximum column widths must equal the spanning cell's maximum width. User agents should divide any changes in column widths equally among the spanned columns.

In addition, the user agent must take into account that when a column width has a percentage value for its `width`, the percentage is calculated in relation to the width of the table—even though that width is not known yet. The user agent must hang on to the percentage value and use it in the next part of the algorithm. Once the user agent has determined how wide or narrow each column can be, it can calculate the width of the table. This happens as follows:

1. If the computed width of the table is not `auto`, the computed table width is compared to the sum of all the column widths plus any borders and cell spacing. (Columns with percentage widths are likely calculated at this time.) The larger of the two values is the final width of the table. If the table's computed width is larger than the sum of the column widths, borders, and cell spacing, all columns are increased in width by an equal amount so they fill the computed width of the table.

2. If the computed width of the table is `auto`, the final width of the table is determined by summing up the column widths, borders, and cell spacing. This means the table will be only as wide as needed to display its content, just as with traditional HTML tables. Any columns with percentage widths use that percentage as a constraint, but it is a constraint that a user agent does not have to satisfy.

Once the last step is completed (and only then), the user agent can actually lay out the table.

Collapsing Cell Borders

The collapsing cell model largely describes how HTML tables have always been laid out when they have no cell spacing. The following rules govern this model:

- Table elements cannot have any padding, although they can have margins. Thus, there is never separation between the border around the outside of the table and its outermost cells.

- Borders can be applied to cells, rows, row groups, columns, and column groups. The table element itself can, as always, have a border.

- There is never any separation between cell borders. In fact, borders collapse into each other where they adjoin so that only one of the collapsing borders is actually drawn. This is somewhat akin to margin collapsing, where the largest margin wins. When cell borders collapse, the "most interesting" border wins.

- Once they are collapsed, the borders between cells are centered on the hypothetical grid lines between the cells.

Collapsing borders

When two or more borders are adjacent, they collapse into each other, as shown in Figure 1-7. There are strict rules governing which borders will win and which will not:

1. If one of the collapsing borders has a border-style of hidden, it takes precedence over all other collapsing borders: all borders at this location are hidden.

2. If one of the collapsing borders has a border-style of none, it takes the lowest priority. There will be no border drawn at this location only if all of the borders meeting at this location have a value of none. Note that none is the default value for border-style.

3. If at least one of the collapsing borders has a value other than either none or hidden, narrow borders lose out to wider ones. If two or more of the collapsing borders have the same width, the border style is taken in the following order, from most preferred to least: double, solid, dashed, dotted, ridge, outset, groove, inset. Thus, if two borders with the same width collapse and one is dashed while the other is outset, the border at that location will be dashed.

4. If collapsing borders have the same style and width but differ in color, the color used is taken from an element in the following list, from most preferred to least: cell, row, row group, column, column group, table. Thus, if the borders of a cell and a column—identical in every way except color—collapse, the cell's border color (and style and width) will be used. If the collapsing borders come from the same type of element—such as two row borders with the same style and width, but different colors—the one farthest to the left and top wins in left-to-right languages; in right-to-left languages, the cell farthest to the right and top wins.

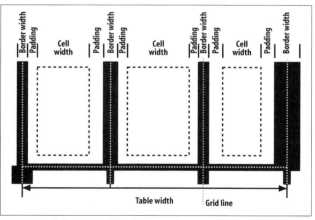

Figure 1-7. Collapsing cell borders model

Vertical Alignment Within Cells

The following describes the detailed process for aligning cell contents within a row:

1. If any of the cells are baseline-aligned, the row's baseline is determined and the content of the baseline-aligned cells is placed.

2. Any top-aligned cell has its content placed. The row now has a provisional height, which is defined by the lowest cell bottom of the cells that have already had their content placed.

3. If any remaining cells are middle- or bottom-aligned, and the content height is taller than the provisional row height, the height of the row is increased by lowering the baseline in order to enclose the tallest of those cells.

4. All remaining cells have their content placed. In any cell with contents shorter than the row height, the cell's padding is increased in order to match the height of the row.

CHAPTER 2

Values

There are a variety of value types in CSS, most of which use units. Combining basic value types (such as numbers) with units (such as pixels) makes it possible to do any number of interesting things with CSS.

Keywords

Keywords are defined on a per-property basis and have a meaning specific only to a given property. For example, `normal` has totally unique meanings for the properties `font-variant` and `letter-spacing`. Keywords, like property names, are not case-sensitive.

CSS defines three "global" keywords that are accepted by every property in the specification:

`inherit`

> Forces the value for the property to be inherited from the element's parent element, even if the property in question is not inherited (e.g., `background-image`). Another way to think of this is that the value is copied from the parent element.

`initial`

> Forces the value of the property to be the initial value defined by the relevant CSS module. For example, `font-style: initial` sets the value of `font-style` to `normal` regardless of the `font-style` value that would have been inherited from the parent element. In cases where the initial value is defined as determined by the user agent, such as for `font-size`, the value is set to the "default" defined by the user agent's preferences.

`unset`

> Combines the effects of both `inherit` and `initial`, with a rudimentary logic built in for good measure. If a property is inherited (e.g., `color`), then `unset` has the same effect as `inherit`. If the property is *not* inherited (e.g., `background-image`), then `unset` has the same effect as `initial`.

If you have a situation where you want to set all of the properties on an element to their default values, thus breaking any chains of inheritance, see the `all` property in Chapter 4.

Color Values

Color values can be expressed in a variety of ways:

#RRGGBB

> This is a hex-pair notation familiar to authors using traditional HTML. In this format, the first pair of digits corresponds to the red level, the second pair to the green, and the third pair to the blue. Each pair is in hexadecimal notation in the range 00–FF (decimal 0–255). Thus, a "pure" blue is written `#0000FF`, a "pure" red is written `#FF0000`, and so on.

#RGB

> This is a shorter form of the six-digit notation described previously. In this format, each digit is replicated to arrive at an equivalent six-digit value; thus, `#F8C` becomes `#FF88CC`.

#RRGGBBAA

An extension of the #RRGGBB notation which adds an alpha channel. As with the R, G, and B values, the A (alpha) value is in hexadecimal notation in the range 00–FF. These are mapped from hexadecimal to decimal in the range 0–1; thus, #00FF0099 is equivalent to the color #00FF00 (light green) with an opacity of 0.6. The opacity here is derived by converting hexadecimal 99 to decimal 153, and then dividing 153 by 255 to get 0.6. Put another way, #00FF0099 is exactly equivalent to rgba(0,255,0,0.6). Note: support for this notation first emerged in early 2016.

#RGBA

This is a shorter form of the eight-digit #RRGGBBAA notation described previously. In this format, each digit is replicated to arrive at an equivalent eight-digit value; thus, #F8C6 becomes #FF88CC66. Note: support for this notation first emerged in early 2016.

rgb(rrr,ggg,bbb)

This format allows the author to use RGB values in the range 0–255; only integers are permitted. Not coincidentally, this range is the decimal equivalent of 00–FF in hexadecimal. In this format, "pure" green is rgb(0,255,0), and white is represented as rgb(255,255,255).

rgb(rrr.rr%,ggg.gg%,bbb.bb%)

This format allows the author to use RGB values in the range 0% to 100%, with decimal values allowed (e.g., 75.5%). The value for black is thus rgb(0%,0%,0%), whereas "pure" blue is rgb(0%,0%,100%).

hsl(hhh.hh,sss.ss%,lll.ll%)

This format permits authors to specify a color by its hue angle, saturation, and lightness (HSL). The hue angle is always a unitless number or a <degree> value in the range 0 to 360, and the saturation and brightness values are always percentages. Hue angles 0 and 360 are equivalent, and are both red. Hue angles greater than 360 can be declared, but they are normalized to the 0–360 range; thus, setting a hue angle of 454 is equivalent to setting an angle of 94. Any HSL value, regardless of color angle, will be rendered as a shade of gray if the saturation value is 0%; the exact shade will depend on the lightness value. Any HSL value, regardless of the hue angle, will be rendered solid black if lightness is 0% and solid white if lightness is 100%. The "normal" lightness value—that is, the value associated with most common colors—is 50%.

rgba(rrr,ggg,bbb,a.aa)
rgba(rrr.rr%,ggg.gg%,bbb.bb%,a.aa)
hsla(hhh.hh,sss.ss%,lll.ll%,a.aa)

These extend the previous three formats to include an alpha (opacity) value. The alpha value must be a real number between 0 and 1 inclusive; percentages are not permitted for the alpha value. Thus, rgba(255,0,0,0.5) and rgba(100%,0%,0%,0.5) and hsla(0,100%,50%,0.5) are all equivalent half-opaque red.

<keyword>

One of 16 recognized keywords based on the original Windows VGA colors. These keywords are aqua, black, blue, fuchsia, gray, green, lime, maroon, navy, olive, purple, red, silver, teal, white, and yellow. Browsers generally also recognize the 148 color keywords documented in the CSS Color Module Level 4 specification (*http://www.w3.org/TR/css-color-4/*), referred to for historical reasons as "the X11 colors" (though the list does not precisely replicate X11's colors).

currentColor

A special keyword that represents the current computed value of the element's color property. This means you can declare background-color: currentColor and set the element's background to be the same color as its foreground (not recommended). When applied to the color property, it is equivalent to declaring color: inherit. It can also be used on borders; border: 1px solid is equivalent to

---

`border: 1px solid currentColor`. This can be quite useful when (un)setting a border's color via DOM scripting.

`transparent`
    A special keyword that is (just barely) a shorthand for `rgba(0,0,0,0)`, which is the computed value any time `transparent` is used.

Number Values

A number value is expressed as a positive or negative number (when permitted). Numbers can be either real (represented as *<number>*) or integers (*<integer>*). They may also restrict the range of acceptable values, as with color values that accept only integers in the range 0–255. A more common range restriction is to limit a number to be non-negative. These are sometimes represented as *<non-negative number>* or *<non-negative integer>*.

Percentage Values

A percentage value is expressed as a *<number>* followed immediately by a percent sign (%). There should never be any space between the number and the percent sign. A percentage value will always be computed relative to something else. For example, declaring `font-size: 120%` for an element sets its font size to 120% of the computed `font-size` of its parent element. Fractional values, such as `543.21%`, are valid. Some properties may restrict percentage values to be non-negative.

Length Values

A length value is expressed as a positive or negative number (when permitted), followed immediately by a unit identifier. There should never be any space between the number and the unit identifier. A length value of 0 (zero) does not require a unit identifier.

Length units are divided into two types: *absolute units*, which are (in theory) always measured in the same way, and *relative units*, which are measured in relation to other things.

Absolute Length Units

The available absolute units are:

Centimeters (`cm`)

> The centimeters found on rulers the world over. There are 2.54 centimeters to an inch, and 1 centimeter equals 0.394 inches. The same mapping warnings that applied to inches also apply to centimeters.

Millimeters (`mm`)

> There are 10 millimeters to a centimeter, so you get 25.4 millimeters to an inch, and 1 millimeter equals 0.0394 inches. Bear in mind the previous warnings about mapping lengths to displays.

Quarter-millimeters (`q`)

> Exactly what they say they are: one-fourth of a millimeter. In other words, 4q equals one millimeter, and 400q equals one centimeter. Again, bear in mind the previous mapping warnings.

Inches (`in`)

> As you might expect, the same inches found on typical US rulers. The mapping from inches to a display device is usually approximate at best, because many systems have no concept of the relation of their display areas to "real-world" measurements such as inches. Thus, inches should be used with extreme caution in screen design.

Points (`pt`)

> Points are standard typographical measures used by printers and typesetters for centuries and by word-processing programs for decades. By modern definition, there are 72 points to an inch. Therefore, the capital letters of text set to 12 points should be 1/6 of an inch tall. For example,

`p {font-size: 18pt;}` is equivalent to `p {font-size: 0.25in;}`, assuming proper mapping of lengths to the display environment (see previous comments).

Picas (`pc`)

Another typographical term. A pica is equivalent to 12 points, which means there are 6 picas to an inch. The capital letters of text set to 1 pica should be 1/6 of an inch tall. For example, `p {font-size: 1.5pc;}` would set text to be the same size as the example declarations found in the definition of points. Keep in mind the previous warnings.

Relative Length Units

The available relative units are:

Em-height (`em`)

This refers to the em-height of a given font face. In CSS, the em-height is equivalent to the height of the character box for the font face, which is to say the computed value of `font-size`. Ems can be used to set relative sizes for fonts; for example, `font-size: 1.2em` is the same as saying `font-size: 120%`.

Root element em-height (`rem`)

Equal to the em-height of the root element (in HTML, the `html` element).

X-height (`ex`)

This refers to the x-height of the font face, which is to say the height of the lowercase "x" character in the given font face. However, the vast majority of font faces do not include their x-height, so many browsers approximate it (poorly) by simply setting `1ex` to be equal to `0.5em`.

ZERO width (`ch`)

This refers to the width of a single zero (Unicode U+0300, "ZERO") in the current font family and size. This is often, but erroneously, assumed to mean "one character." This will only be true in monospace fonts, where all characters are the same width. Since most proportional fonts have zeros that are slimmer than the alphabetic symbols, setting something like width: 60ch will often result in lines of text with fewer than 60 characters.

Pixels (px)

A pixel is usually thought of as a small box on a display, but CSS defines pixels more abstractly. In CSS terms, a pixel is defined to be about the size required to yield 96 units per inch. Many user agents ignore this definition in favor of simply addressing the pixels on the display, but others (such as those on high-resolution mobile devices) go the CSS route, treating each px as being multiple physical on-screen pixels.

Viewport width unit (vw)

This unit is calculated with respect to the viewport's width, which is divided by 100. If the viewport is 937 pixels wide, for example, 1vw is equal to 9.37px. If the viewport's width changes, say by dragging the browser window to be wider or narrower, the value of vw changes along with it.

Viewport height unit (vh)

This unit is calculated with respect to the viewport's height, which is divided by 100. If the viewport is 650 pixels tall, for example, 1vh is equal to 6.5px. If the viewport's height changes, say by dragging the browser window to be taller or shorter, the value of vh changes along with it.

Viewport minimum unit (vmin)

This unit is 1/100 of the viewport's width or height, whichever is *lesser*. Thus, given a viewport that is 937 pixels wide by 650 pixels tall, 1vmin is equal to 6.5px.

Viewport maximum unit (vmax)

This unit is 1/100 of the viewport's width or height, whichever is *greater*. Thus, given a viewport that is 937 pixels wide by 650 pixels tall, 1vmax is equal to 9.37px.

Fraction Values

A *fraction value* is a *<number>* followed by the label `fr`. Thus, one fraction unit is `1fr`, four fraction units are `4fr`, and so on. This is a concept introduced by Grid Layout, and is used to divide up fractions of the unconstrained space in a layout. Note that `fr` is *not* a *<length>* unit, and thus cannot be used in places where length values are permitted (e.g., `calc()` expressions, see "Calculation Values" on page 45).

URIs

A URI value (*<uri>*) is a reference to a file such as a graphic or another stylesheet. CSS defines a URI as relative to the stylesheet that contains it. URI stands for Uniform Resource Identifier, which is the more recent name for URLs. (Technically, URLs are a subset of URIs.) In CSS, which was first defined when URIs were still called URLs, this means that references to URIs will often appear in the form `url(<uri>)`. Fun!

Angles

The format of an *<angle>* is expressed as a *<number>* followed immediately by an angle unit. There are four types of angle units: degrees (`deg`), grads (`grad`), radians (`rad`), and turns (`turn`). For example, a right angle could be declared as `90deg`, `100grad`, `1.571rad`, or `0.25turn`. In each case, the values are translated into degrees in the range 0 through 360. This is also true of negative values: `-90deg` is equivalent to `270deg`.

Times

A time value (*<time>*) is expressed as a *<number>* followed immediately by a time unit. There are two types of time units: seconds (`s`) and milliseconds (`ms`). Time values appear in aural styles, which are not widely supported, and in the much better-supported transitions and animations.

Frequencies

A frequency value (*<frequency>*) is expressed as a non-negative *<number>* followed immediately by a frequency unit. There are two types of frequency units: hertz (Hz) and kilohertz (kHz). The unit identifiers are case-insensitive, so 6kHz and 6khz are equivalent. As of this writing, frequency values are only used with aural styles, which are not well supported.

Position

A position value (*<position>*) is how you specify the placement of an origin image in backgrounds, object fitting, masking placement, and a few other circumstances. Its syntactical structure is rather complicated:

```
[
  [ left | center | right | top | bottom | <percentage> | <length> ] ] |
  [ left | center | right | <percentage> | <length> ]
  [ top | center | bottom | <percentage> | <length> ] ] |
  [ center | [ left | right ] [ <percentage> | <length> ]? ] &&
  [ center | [ top | bottom ] [ <percentage> | <length> ]? ]
]
```

That might seem a little convoluted and repetitive, but it's all down to the subtly complex patterns that this value type has to allow, such as center, bottom right, 50% center, left 77px, and so on. The notation used here is described in "Value Syntax Conventions" on page 73.

Strings

A string (*<string>*) is a series of characters enclosed by either single or double quotes. If a string needs to include the same quote that encloses it, it must be escaped. For example, 'That\'s amazing!' or "Deploy the \"scare quotes\" at once!". If a newline is needed within a string, it is represented as \A, which is the Unicode codepoint for the line feed character. Any Unicode character can be represented using an escaped codepoint reference; thus, a left curly double quotation mark can be represented with \201C. If a string does contain a line feed for legibility reasons, it must be escaped and will be removed when processing the string.

Identifiers

There are some properties that accept an *identifier value*, which is a user-defined label of some kind; the most common examples are grid lines and areas in grid layout and keyframe names in animations. Identifiers are represented in the value syntax as *<identifier>*. Identifiers are words and are case-sensitive; thus, myID and MyID are, as far as CSS is concerned, completely distinct and unrelated to each other. In cases where a property accepts both an identifier and one or more keywords, the author should take care to never define an identifier identical to a valid keyword.

Attribute Values

In a few CSS properties, it's possible to pull in the value of an HTML attribute defined for the element being styled. This is done with the attr() value. As of early 2018, this is almost exclusively done with generated content, using the content property.

For example, h2::before {content: "[" attr(ID) "] ";} will insert an opening square bracket, the ID of the h2 element, and then a closing square bracket and trailing space. Any attribute, including HTML data-* attributes, can be addressed in this manner.

Calculation Values

Calculation values take the form calc(), with an equation inside the parentheses. calc() can be used wherever *<length>*, *<frequency>*, *<angle>*, *<time>*, *<percentage>*, *<number>*, or *<integer>* values are allowed. You can also use all these unit types within a calc() value, though there are some limitations to keep in mind.

Inside the parentheses, you can construct simple mathematical expressions. The permitted operators are + (addition), - (subtraction), * (multiplcation), and / (division), as well as parentheses. These follow the traditional PEMDAS (parentheses, exponents, multiplication, division, addition, subtraction) precedence order—although in this case it's really just PMDAS, since as of early 2018, exponents are not permitted in calc().

The basic limitation is that calc() does simple type-checking to make sure that units are compatible:

1. To either side of a + or - operator, both values must have the same unit type or must both be *<number>* and/or *<integer>* values (in which case, the result is a *<number>*).

2. Given a * operator, one of the values involved must be a *<number>* (which, remember, includes *<integer>* values).

3. Given a / operator, the value on the *right* side must be a *<number>*. If the left-side value is an *<integer>*, the result is a *<number>*. Otherwise, the result is of the unit used on the left side.

4. Any circumstance that creates division by zero makes the value invalid.

There's one more notable limitation: whitespace is *required* to either side of the + and - operators, while it is not for * and /. This avoids ambiguity with respect to numeric values, which can be negative.

Variable Values

As this book was being finished in early 2018, a new capability was being added to CSS. The technical term for this is *custom properties*, even though what these really do is create (sort of) variables in your CSS. They do not, contrary to their name, create special CSS properties, in the sense of properties like color or font.

Custom properties are defined by giving a custom identifier a value, like this:

```
html {
    --mainColor: #AEA434;
}
```

The important thing is that any custom identifier of this type begins with *two* hyphens (--). Anything else, and the identifier will not be recognized, meaning the variable definition will fail.

The defined value can then be invoked later on using a var() value type, like this:

```
h1 {color: var(--mainColor);}
```

Note that these names are case-sensitive, so --maincolor and --MainColor are completely separate identifiers. Custom properties are scoped to the element to which they are applied.

Selectors and Queries

Selectors

Universal Selector

Pattern	`*`
Description	Matches any element name in the document's language. If a rule does not have an explicit selector, the universal selector is inferred.
Examples	`* {color: red;}` `div * p {color: blue;}`

Type Selector

Pattern	`element1`
Description	Matches the name of an element in the document's language. Every instance of the element name is matched. (CSS1 referred to these as "element selectors.")
Examples	`body {background: #FFF;}` `p {font-size: 1em;}`

Descendant Selector

Pattern   `element1 element2 ...`

Description   Matches elements based on their status as a descendant of another element. The matched element can be a child, grandchild, great-grandchild, etc. of the ancestor element. (CSS1 referred to these as "contextual selectors.")

Examples
```
body h1 {font-size: 200%;}
table tr td div ul li {color: purple;}
```

Child Selector

Pattern   `element1 > element2`

Description   Matches an element based on its status as a child of another element. It is more restrictive than a descendant selector, as only a child will be matched.

Examples
```
div > p {color: cyan;}
ul > li {font-weight: bold;}
```

Adjacent Sibling Selector

Pattern   `element1 + element2`

Description   Matches an element that is the following adjacent sibling of another element. (Sibling elements, as the name implies, share the same parent element.) Any anonymous text nodes between the two elements are ignored; only elements and their positions in the document tree are considered.

Examples
```
table + p {margin-top: 2.5em;}
h1 + * {margin-top: 0;}
```

General Sibling Selector

Pattern   `element1 ~ element2`

Description   Matches an element that is a sibling of another element which it follows in the document tree. Any text or other elements between the two elements are ignored; only the elements and their positions in the document tree are considered.

Examples

```
h1 ~ h2 {margin-top: 2.5em;}
nav a ~ a {border-left: 1px solid border;}
```

Class Selector

Pattern

```
element1.classname
element1.classname1.classname2
```

Description

In languages that permit it, such as HTML, SVG, and MathML, a class selector using "dot notation" matches elements that have a class attribute containing a specific value or values. The name of the class value must immediately follow the dot. Multiple class values can be chained together. If no element name precedes the dot, the selector matches all elements bearing that class value or values.

Examples

```
p.urgent {color: red;}
a.external {font-style: italic;}
.example {background: olive;}
.note.caution {background: yellow;}
```

ID Selector

Pattern

```
element1#idname
```

Description

In languages that permit it, such as HTML or SVG, an ID selector selects elements that have an id attribute containing a specific value. The name of the ID value must immediately follow the octothorpe (#). If no element name precedes the octothorpe, the selector matches all elements containing that ID value.

Examples

```
h1#page-title {font-size: 250%;}
body#home {background: silver;}
#example {background: lime;}
```

Simple Attribute Selector

Pattern   element1[attr]

Description   Matches elements based on the presence of an attribute, regardless of the attribute's value.

Examples
```
a[rel] {border-bottom: 3px double gray;}
p[class] {border: 1px dotted silver;}
```

Exact Attribute Value Selector

Pattern   element1[attr="value"]

Description   Matches elements based on the precise and complete value of an attribute.

Examples
```
a[rel="start"] {font-weight: bold;}
p[class="urgent"] {color: red;}
```

Partial Attribute Value Selector

Pattern   element1[attr~="value"]

Description   Matches elements based on a portion of the space-separated value of an attribute. Note that [class~="*value*"] is equivalent to .*value* (see above).

Examples
```
a[rel~="friend"] {text-transform: uppercase;}
p[class~="warning"] {background: yellow;}
```

Beginning Substring Attribute Value Selector

Pattern   element1[attr^="substring"]

Description   Matches elements based on a substring at the very beginning of an attribute's value.

Examples
```
a[href^="/blog"] {text-transform: uppercase;}
p[class^="test-"] {background: yellow;}
```

Ending Substring Attribute Value Selector

Pattern   `element1[attr$="substring"]`

Description Matches elements based on a substring at the very end of an attribute's value.

Example   `a[href$=".pdf"] {font-style: italic;}`

Arbitrary Substring Attribute Value Selector

Pattern   `element1[attr*="substring"]`

Description Matches elements based on a substring found anywhere within an attribute's value.

Examples   `a[href*="oreilly.com"] {font-weight: bold;}`
`div[class*="port"] {border: 1px solid red;}`

Language Attribute Selector

Pattern   `element1[lang|="language-identifier"]`

Description Matches elements with a `lang` attribute whose value is one of a hyphen-separated list of values, starting with the value provided in the selector.

In an HTML document, the language of an element is determined by its `lang` attribute. If an element does not have one, its language is determined by the `lang` attribute of its nearest ancestor that does have one, or, lacking that, by the `Content-Language` HTTP header response field (or the respective `meta http-equiv`) for the document.

Example   `html[lang|="tr"] {color: red;}`

Structural Pseudo-Classes

Strictly speaking, all pseudo-classes (like all selectors) are structural: they are, after all, dependent on document structure in some fashion. What sets the pseudo-classes listed here apart is that they are intrinsically about patterns found in the structure of the document: for example, selecting every other paragraph or elements that are the last children of their parent element.

:empty

Applies to   Any element

Description   Matches elements that have no child nodes—that is, no child elements *or* content nodes. Content nodes are defined as any text, whitespace, entity reference, or CDATA nodes. Thus, `<p> </p>` is *not* empty because it has a single whitespace character inside it; nor is the element empty if that space is replaced with a newline. Note that this pseudo-class does *not* apply to empty elements such as `<br>`, `<img>`, `<input>`, and so on.

Examples
```
p:empty {padding: 1em; background: red;}
div:not(:empty) {border: 1px solid;
    padding: 1ch;}
li:empty {display: none;}
```

:first-child

Applies to   Any element

Description   Matches an element when it is the first child of another element. Thus, `div:first-child` will select any div that is the first child of another element, *not* the first child element of any div.

Examples
```
td:first-child {border-left: 1px solid;}
p:first-child {text-indent: 0; margin-top: 2em;}
```

:first-of-type

Applies to   Any element

Description   Matches an element when it is the first child of its type, as compared to all its sibling elements. Thus, `div:first-of-type` will select any div that is the first child div of another element.

Examples	`td:first-of-type {border-left: 1px dotted;}` `h2:first-of-type {color: fuchsia;}`

:lang

Applies to	Any element with associated language-encoding information.
Description	Matches elements based on their human-language encoding. Such language information must be contained within, or otherwise associated with, the document—it cannot be assigned from CSS. The handling of :lang is the same as for |= attribute selectors.
Examples	`html:lang(en) {background: silver;}` `*:lang(fr) {quotes: '&#171;' '&#187;';}`

:last-child

Applies to	Any element
Description	Matches an element when it is the last child of another element. Thus, div:last-child will select any div that is the last child of another element, *not* the last child element of any div.
Examples	`td:last-child {border-right: 1px solid;}` `p:last-child {margin-bottom: 2em;}`

:last-of-type

Applies to	Any element
Description	Matches an element when it is the last child of its type, as compared to all its sibling elements. Thus, div:last-of-type will select any div that is the last child div of another element.
Examples	`td:last-of-type {border-right: 1px dotted;}` `h2:last-of-type {color: fuchsia;}`

:nth-child(*a*n±*b*)

Applies to   Any element

Description   Matches every *n*th child with the pattern of selection defined by the formula *a*n±*b*, where *a* and *b* are <*integer*>s and n represents an infinite series of integers, counting forward from the first child. Thus, to select every fourth child of the body element, starting with the first child, you would write body > *:nth-child(4n+1). This will select the first, fifth, ninth, fourteenth, and so on children of the body.

If you literally wish to select the fourth, eighth, twelfth, and so on children, you can modify the selector to body > *:nth-child(4n). It is also possible for *b* to be negative: body > *:nth-child(4n-1) selects the third, seventh, eleventh, fifteenth, and so on children of the body.

In place of the *a*n±*b* formula, there are two keywords permitted: even and odd. These are equivalent to 2n and 2n+1, respectively.

Examples   `*:nth-child(4n+1) {font-weight: bold;}`
`tbody tr:nth-child(odd) {background-color: #EEF;}`

:nth-last-child(*a*n±*b*)

Applies to   Any element

Description   Matches every *n*th child with the pattern of selection defined by the formula *a*n±*b*, where *a* and *b* are <*integer*>s and n represents an infinite series of integers, *counting backward from the last child*. Thus, to select every fourth-to-last child of the body element, starting with the last child, you would write body > *:nth-last-child(4n+1). This is, in effect, the mirror image of :nth-child.

In place of the *a*n±*b* formula, there are two keywords permitted: even and odd. These are equivalent to 2n and 2n+1, respectively.

Examples   ```
                        *:nth-last-child(4n+1) {font-weight: bold;}
                        tbody tr:nth-last-child(odd) {
                            background-color: #EEF;}
                        ```

---

# :nth-last-of-type(*an*±*b*)

**Applies to**          Any element

**Description**         Matches every *n*th child that is of the same type as
                        the element named, with the pattern of selection
                        defined by the formula *an*±*b*, where *a* and *b* are
                        <*integer*>s and n represents an infinite series of inte-
                        gers, *counting backward from the last such element*.
                        Thus, to select every third-to-last paragraph (p) that
                        is a child of the body element, starting with the first
                        such paragraph, you would write body > p:nth-
                        last-of-type(3n+1). This holds true even if other
                        elements (e.g., lists, tables, or other elements) are
                        interspersed between the various paragraphs.

                        In place of the *an*±*b* formula, there are two key-
                        words permitted: even and odd. These are equiva-
                        lent to 2n and 2n+1, respectively.

**Examples**            ```
                        td:nth-last-of-type(even) {
                            background-color: #FCC;}
                        img:nth-last-of-type(3n) {float: left;
                            border: 2px solid;}
                        ```

:nth-of-type(*an*±*b*)

Applies to   Any element

Description   Matches every *n*th child that is of the same type as
                        the element named, with the pattern of selection
                        defined by the formula *an*±*b*, where *a* and *b* are
                        <*integer*>s and n represents an infinite series of inte-
                        gers, counting forward from the first such element.
                        Thus, to select every third paragraph (p) that is a
                        child of the body element, starting with the first such
                        paragraph, you would write body > p:nth-of-
                        type(3n+1). This will select the first, fourth,

seventh, tenth, and so on child paragraphs of the body. This holds true even if other elements (e.g., lists, tables, or other elements) are interspersed between the various paragraphs.

In place of the $an \pm b$ formula, there are two keywords permitted: even and odd. These are equivalent to 2n and 2n+1, respectively.

Examples ```
td:nth-of-type(even) {background-color: #FCC;}
img:nth-of-type(3n) {float: right;}
```

## :only-child

**Applies to**  Any element

**Description**  Matches an element that is the only child element of its parent element. A common use case for this selector is to remove the border from any linked image, assuming that image is the only element in the link. Note that an element can be selected by :only-child even if it has its own child or children. It must simply be the only child of its parent.

**Examples**  ```
a img:only-child {border: 0;}
table div:only-child {margin: 5px;}
```

:only-of-type

Applies to Any element

Description Matches an element that is the only child element of its type of its parent element. Note that an element can be selected by :only-of-type even if it has its own child or children of its own type (such as divs within a div).

Examples ```
p em:only-of-type {font-weight: bold;}
section article:only-of-type {margin: 2em 0 3em;}
```

## :root

**Applies to**  The root element
```

Description	This matches the document's root element, which in HTML is always the html element. In SVG, it is the svg element. In XML formats, the root element can have any name; thus, a generic root-element selector is needed.
Examples	`:root {font: medium serif;}` `:root > * {margin: 1.5em 0;}`

The Negation Pseudo-Class

There is but one pseudo-class that handles negation, but it is so unique that it deserves its own subsection.

:not(*e*)

Applies to	Any element
Description	Matches every element that is *not* described by the simple selector *e*. For example, you can select every element that is not a paragraph by stating `*:not(p)`.
	More usefully, negation can be used within the context of descendant selectors. An example of this would be selecting every element within a table that is not a data cell using `table *:not(td)`. Another example would be selecting every element with an ID that is not search by using `[id]:not([id="search"])`.
	Note that there is one exception to the "simple selector" definition of *e*: it cannot be a negation pseudo-class itself. That is, it is impermissible to write `:not(:not(div))`.
	Because `:not()` is a pseudo-class, it can be chained with other pseudo-classes as well as with instances of itself. For example, to select any focused element that isn't an a element, use `*:focus:not(a)`. To select any element that isn't either a paragraph or a section, use `*:not(p):not(section)`.

As of early 2018, the "simple selector" restriction means that grouped, descendant, and combined selectors are not permitted within :not() expressions. This restriction is being loosened in CSS Selectors Level 4.

Examples
```
ul *:not(li) {text-indent: 2em;}
*:not([type="checkbox"]):not([type="radio"]) {
    margin: 0 1em;}
```

Interaction Pseudo-Classes

The pseudo-classes listed here are all related to the user's interaction with the document: whether styling different link states, highlighting an element that's the target of a fragment identifier, or styling form elements based on their being enabled or disabled.

:active

Applies to   Any interaction element

Description   Matches an element during the period in which it is being activated. The most common example is clicking on a hyperlink in an HTML document: while the mouse button is being held down, the link is active. There are other ways to activate elements, and other elements can in theory be activated, although CSS doesn't define them.

Examples
```
a:active {color: red;}
*:active {background: blue;}
```

:checked

Applies to   Any interaction element that has an on/off state

Description   Matches any user interface element that has been "toggled on," such as a checked checkbox or a filled radio button.

Examples
```
input:checked {
    outline: 3px solid rgba(127,127,127,0.5);}
```

```
input[type="checkbox"]:checked {
  box-shadow: red 0 0 5px;}
```

:disabled

Applies to   Any interaction element

Description   Matches user interface elements that are not able to
accept user input because of language attributes or
other nonpresentational means; for example, <input
type="text"   disabled>   in   HTML5.   Note
that :disabled does *not* apply when an input element has simply been removed from the viewport
with properties like position or display.

Example   `input:disabled {opacity: 0.5;}`

:enabled

Applies to   Any interaction element

Description   Matches user interface elements that are able to
accept user input and that can be set to "enabled"
and "disabled" states through the markup language
itself. This includes any form input element in
(X)HTML, but does not include hyperlinks.

Example   `input:enabled {background: #FCC;}`

:focus

Applies to   Any interaction element

Description   Matches an element during the period in which it
has focus. One example from HTML is an input box
that has the text-input cursor within it such that
when the user starts typing, text will be entered into
that box. Other elements, such as hyperlinks, can
also have focus; however, CSS does not define which
elements may or may not have focus.

Examples   `a:focus {outline: 1px dotted red;}`
`input:focus {background: yellow;}`

:hover

Applies to   Any interaction element

Description   Matches an element during the period in which it is
being *hovered* over (when the user is designating an
element without activating it). The most common
example of this is moving the mouse pointer inside
the boundaries of a hyperlink in an HTML document. Other elements can in theory be hovered over,
although CSS doesn't define which ones.

Examples   `a[href]:hover {text-decoration: underline;}`
`p:hover {background: yellow;}`

:link

Applies to   A hyperlink to a resource that has not been visited

Description   Matches a link to a URI that has not been visited;
that is, the URI to which the link points does not
appear in the user agent's history. This state is mutu-
ally exclusive with the `:visited` state.

Examples   `a:link {color: blue;}`
`*:link {text-decoration: underline;}`

:target

Applies to   Any element

Description   Matches an element which is itself matched by the
fragment identifier portion of the URI used to
access the page. Thus, `http://www.w3.org/TR/`
`css3-selectors/#target-pseudo`   would   be
matched by `:target` and would apply the declared
styles to any element with the `id` of `target-pseudo`.
If that element was a paragraph, it would also be
matched by `p:target`.

Example   `:target {background: #EE0;}`

:visited

Applies to	A hyperlink to a resource that has already been visited
Description	Matches a link to a URI that has been visited; that is, the URI to which the link points appears in the user agent's history. This state is mutually exclusive with the :link state.
Examples	`a:visited {color: purple;}` `*:visited {color: gray;}`

Pseudo-Elements

In CSS1 and CSS2, pseudo-elements were preceded by single colons, just as pseudo-classes were. In CSS3 and later, pseudo-elements use double colons to distinguish them from pseudo-classes. For historical reasons, browsers will support both single and double colons on pseudo-elements, but the double-colon syntax is recommended.

::after

Generates	A pseudo-element containing generated content placed after the content in the element
Description	Inserts generated content at the end of an element's content. By default, the pseudo-element is inline, but this can be changed using the property `display`.

Examples	`a.external:after {`
	`    content: " " url(/icons/globe.gif);}`
	`p:after {content: " |; ";}`

::before

Generates	A pseudo-element containing generated content placed before the content in the element
Description	Inserts generated content at the beginning of an element's content. By default, the pseudo-element is

inline, but this can be changed using the property
display.

Examples
```
a[href]:before {content: "[LINK] ";}
p:before {content: attr(class);}
a[rel|;="met"]:after {content: " *";}
```

::first-letter

Generates   A pseudo-element that contains the first letter of an
element

Description   Styles the first letter of an element. Any leading
punctuation should be styled along with the first letter. Some languages have letter combinations that
should be treated as a single character, and a user
agent may apply the first letter style to both. Prior to
CSS2.1, ::first-letter could be attached only to
block-level elements. CSS2.1 expanded its scope to
include elements with a display value of block,
list-item, table-cell, table-caption, or inline-
block. There is a limited set of properties that can
apply to a first letter.

Examples
```
h1:first-letter {font-size: 166%;}
p:first-letter {text-decoration: underline;}
```

::first-line

Generates   A pseudo-element that contains the first formatted
line of an element

Description   Styles the first line of text in an element, regardless
of how many or how few words may appear in that
line. ::first-line can be attached only to block-
level elements. There is a limited set of properties
that can apply to a first line.

Example
```
p.lead:first-line {font-weight: bold;}
```

Media Queries

With media queries, an author can define the media environment in which a given stylesheet, or portion of a stylesheet, is used by the browser. In the past, this was handled by setting media types with the media attribute on link elements, or with the media descriptor on @import declarations. Media queries take this concept several steps further by allowing authors to choose stylesheets based on the features of a given media type.

Basic Concepts

The placement of media queries will be very familiar to any author who has ever set a media type. Here are two ways of applying an external stylesheet when rendering the document on a color printer:

```
<link href="print-color.css" type="text/css"
 media="print and (color)" rel="stylesheet">

@import url(print-color.css) print and (color);
```

Anywhere a media type can be used, a media query can be used. This means that it is possible to list more than one query in a comma-separated list:

```
<link href="print-color.css" type="text/css"
 media="print and (color), projection and (color)"
 rel="stylesheet">

@import url(print-color.css) print and (color),
 projection and (color);
```

In any situation where one of the media queries evaluates to true, the associated stylesheet is applied. Thus, given the previous @import, *print-color.css* will be applied if rendering to a color printer or a color projection environment. If printing on a black-and-white printer, both queries will evaluate to false and *print-color.css* will not be applied to the document. The same holds for any screen medium, a grayscale projection environment, an aural media environment, and so forth.

Each query is composed of a media type and one or more listed media features. Each media feature is enclosed in parentheses, and multiple features are linked with the and keyword. There are two logical keywords in media queries:

and

> Links together two or more media features in such a way that all of them must be true for the query to be true. For example, (color) and (orientation: landscape) and (min-device-width: 800px) means that all three conditions must be satisfied: if the media environment has color, and is in landscape orientation, and the device's display is at least 800 pixels wide, the stylesheet is used.

not

> Negates the entire query so that if all of the conditions are true, the stylesheet is *not* applied. For example, not (color) and (orientation: landscape) and (min-device-width: 800px) means that if the three conditions are satisfied, the statement is negated. Thus, if the media environment has color, and is in landscape orientation, and the device's display is at least 800 pixels wide, the stylesheet is *not* used. In all other cases, it will be used. Note that the not keyword can only be used at the beginning of a media query. It is *not* legal to write something like (color) and not (min-device-width: 800px). In such cases, the query will be ignored. Note also that browsers too old to understand media queries will always skip a stylesheet whose media descriptor starts with not.

There is no or keyword for use within a given query, but the commas that separate a list of queries serve the function of an or; that is, screen, print means "apply if the media is screen or print." Thus, instead of screen and (max-color: 2) or (monochrome), which is invalid and thus ignored, you should write screen and (max-color: 2), screen and (monochrome).

There is one more keyword, only, which is designed to create deliberate backward incompatibility.

`only`

Used to hide a stylesheet from browsers too old to understand media queries. For example, to apply a stylesheet in all media, but only in those browsers that understand media queries, you would write something like `@import url(new.css) only all`. In browsers that do understand media queries, the `only` keyword is ignored. Note that the `only` keyword can be used only at the beginning of a media query.

Media Query Values

There are two new value types introduced by media queries, which (as of early 2018) are not used in any other context:

<ratio>

A ratio value is two positive *<integer>* values separated by a solidus (/) and optional whitespace. The first value refers to the width, and the second to the height. Thus, to express a width-to-height ratio of 16:9, you can write `16/9` or `16 / 9`.

<resolution>

A resolution value is a positive *<integer>* followed by either of the unit identifiers `dpi` or `dpcm`. As usual, whitespace is not permitted between the *<integer>* and the identifier.

Media Features

As of early 2018, the available media features are as follows. Note that their values cannot be negative:

`width, min-width, max-width`
Values: <length>

Refers to the width of the display area of the user agent. In a screen-media web browser, this is the width of the viewport plus any scrollbars. In paged media, this is the width of the page box. Thus, (`min-`

width: 850px) applies when the viewport is greater
than 850 pixels wide.

`device-width, min-device-width, max-device-width`
Values: <length>

Refers to the width of the complete rendering area of
the output device. In screen media, this is the width
of the screen. In paged media, this is the width of the
page. Thus, (`max-device-width: 1200px`) applies
when the device's output area is less than 1,200 pixels
wide.

`height, min-height, max-height`
Values: <length>

Refers to the height of the display area of the user
agent. In a screen-media web browser, this is the
height of the viewport plus any scrollbars. In paged
media, this is the height of the page box. Thus,
(`height: 567px`) applies when the viewport's height is
precisely 567 pixels tall.

`device-height, min-device-height, max-device-height`
Values: <length>

Refers to the height of the complete rendering area of
the output device. In screen media, this is the height
of the screen. In paged media, this is the height of the
page. Thus, (`max-device-height: 400px`) applies
when the device's output area is less than 400 pixels
tall.

`aspect-ratio, min-aspect-ratio, max-aspect-ratio`
Values: <ratio>

Refers to the ratio that results from comparing the
`width` media feature to the `height` media feature (see
the definition of *<ratio>*). Thus, (`min-aspect-ratio:
2/1`) applies to any viewport whose width-to-height
ratio is at least 2:1.

`device-aspect-ratio`, `min-device-aspect-ratio`, `max-device-aspect-ratio`

Values: <length>

Refers to the ratio that results from comparing the `device-width` media feature to the `device-height` media feature (see the definition of *<ratio>*). Thus, (`device-aspect-ratio: 16/9`) applies to any output device whose display area width-to-height ratio is exactly 16:9.

`color`, `min-color`, `max-color`

Values: <integer>

Refers to the presence of color-display capability in the output device, with an optional number representing the number of bits used in each color component. Thus, (`color`) applies to any device with any color depth at all, whereas (`min-color: 4`) means there must be at least four bits used per color component. Any device that does not support color will return 0.

`color-index`, `min-color-index`, `max-color-index`

Values: <integer>

Refers to the total number of colors available in the output device's color lookup table. Thus, (`min-color-index: 256`) applies to any device with a minimum of 256 colors available. Any device that does not use a color lookup table will return 0.

`monochrome`, `min-monochrome`, `max-monochrome`

Values: <integer>

Refers to the presence of a monochrome display, with an optional number of bits per pixel in the output device's frame buffer. Thus, (`monochrome`) applies to any monochrome output device, whereas (`min-monochrome: 2`) applies to any monochrome output device with a minimum of two bits per pixel in the frame buffer. Any device that is not monochrome will return 0.

resolution, min-resolution, max-resolution
> *Values:* <resolution>
>> Refers to the resolution of the output device in terms of pixel density, measured in either dots per inch (dpi) or dots per centimeter (dpcm). If an output device has pixels that are not square, the least dense axis is used; for example, if a device is 100dpcm along one axis and 120dpcm along the other, 100dpcm is the value returned. Additionally, a bare resolution feature query can never match (though min-resolution and max-resolution can).

orientation
> *Values:* portrait | landscape
>> Refers to the output device's total output area, where portrait is returned if the media feature height is equal to or greater than the media feature width. Otherwise, the result is landscape.

scan
> *Values:* progressive | interlace
>> Refers to the scanning process used in an output device with a media type of tv.

grid
> *Values:* 0 | 1
>> Refers to the presence (or absence) of a grid-based output device, such as a tty terminal. A grid-based device will return 1; otherwise, 0 is returned.

Feature Queries

A *feature query* is an at-rule block similar to a media query. The difference is that it queries a user agent about its support for a given property-value combination. If the user agent indicates it supports the query, the rules within the at-block are applied. Otherwise, they are ignored.

A basic example is to ask the browser if it supports background-color: red:

```
@supports (background-color: red) {
    html {background-color: yellow;}
    body {background-color: white;}
}
```

There is no obligation to use the property-value combination in the query in the subsequent rules. In fact, there's no obligation even to use the property that was part of the feature query. You can ask if a browser supports color: #FFF and then write rules that never touch color. (But just because you can doesn't mean you should.)

Feature queries are useful when applying advanced CSS features. For example, converting a float-based layout to grid might look something like this:

```
[...float layout rules here…]

@supports (display: grid) {
    [...grid layout rules here…]
    [...rules that turn off margins, clearing,
      and other rules needed for float layout
      but not in grid layout…]
}
```

It's also possible to do a negated feature query using the keyword not:

```
@supports not (shape-outside: circle()) {
    [...rules for use in browsers that don't understand
      circle float shapes…]
}
```

Property Reference

Inheritance and Animation

Each property listed in this chapter has "Inh." and "Anim." values. The values "N" (for no) and "Y" (for yes) indicate whether a property is *inherited* by descendant elements and whether the property is *animatable*, or able to be affected using the various animation and transition properties. In cases where only some of a property's values are animatable, the value given will be "P" (for partial) and more details will be given in the property's definition.

Value Syntax Conventions

Any words presented in `constant width` are keywords that must appear literally, without quotes. The forward slash (/) and the comma (,) must also be used literally.

Any italicized words between "<" and ">" give a type of value, or a reference to another property's values. For example, the property `font` accepts values that originally belong to the property `font-family`. This is denoted by using the text *<font-family>*. Similarly, if a value type like a color is permitted, it will be represented using *<color>*.

There are a number of ways to combine components of a value definition:

- Two or more keywords strung together with only space separating them means that all of them must occur in the given order.

- If a vertical bar separates alternatives (X | Y), then any one of them must occur, but only one.

- A vertical double bar (X ‖ Y) means that X, Y, or both must occur, but they may appear in any order.

- A double ampersand (X && Y) means both X and Y must occur, though they may appear in any order.

- Brackets ([...]) group things together. Thus "[please ‖ help ‖ me] do this" means that one or more of the words please, help, and me must appear (in any order, and at most once). do this must always appear, with those words in that order.

Every component or bracketed group may (or may not) be followed by one of these modifiers:

- An asterisk (*) indicates that the preceding value or bracketed group is repeated zero or more times.

- A plus (+) indicates that the preceding value or bracketed group is repeated one or more times.

- An octothorp (#) indicates that the preceding value or bracketed group is repeated one or more times, separated by commas as needed.

- A question mark (?) indicates that the preceding value or bracketed group is optional.

- An exclamation point (!) indicates that the preceding value or bracketed group is required, and thus must result in at least one value, even if the syntax would seem to indicate otherwise.

- A pair of numbers in curly braces ({M,N}) indicates that the preceding value or bracketed group is repeated at least M and at most N times.

Universal Values

Any user agent that has fully implemented the Cascading and Inheritance module will honor the following values for all properties. Think of it as a given property's value syntax being written something like:

[*(listed value syntax)*] | inherit | initial | unset

These three keywords are not listed in the following property definitions, for purposes of clarity. The exception is the property all, which accepts *only* these three keywords as values. For definitions of these keywords' meaning, see Chapter 2.

Properties

align-content   Inh. N   Anim. N

Values	flex-start | flex-end | center | space-between | space-around | space-evenly | stretch
Initial value	stretch
Computed value	As declared
Applies to	Flex containers
Description	Defines the distribution of flex lines along the cross axis of a flex container, given that the container's cross-axis length does not equal the sum of the flex lines' size along the same axis.
Examples	aside {display: flex; align-content: center;} section {display: flex; height: 90vh; align-content: flex-end;}
Note	As of early 2018, there are plans to have this property apply to many (or all) elements, not just flex

containers, and be given the values start and end to replicate flex-start and flex-end behavior for non-flex environments. Thanks to the center value, this change would make vertical centering of content trivial in nearly all cases.

align-items   Inh. N Anim. N

Values	flex-start | flex-end | center | baseline | stretch
Initial value	stretch
Computed value	As declared
Applies to	Flex containers, grid containers, and multicolumn containers
Description	Sets a flex-container-wide default for items' alignment with respect to the cross axis of the flex line they occupy. baseline alignment means the items in a line are all placed such that the baselines of their first lines of text line up.
Examples	div.flexy {align-items: flex-start;} section.gallery {align-items: baseline;}
Note	As of early 2018, there are plans to have this property apply to many (or all) elements and be given the values start and end to replicate flex-start and flex-end behavior for non-flex environments.

align-self   Inh. N Anim. N

Values	flex-start | flex-end | center | baseline | stretch
Initial value	stretch
Computed value	As declared
Applies to	Flex and grid items
Description	Sets the alignment for a single item with respect to the cross axis of the flex line it occupies. baseline

alignment means the baseline of the item's first line of text is aligned with the lowest first-line baseline in the flex line.

Examples	`div.flexy .midpointed {align-self: center;}` `section.gallery h1 {align-self: stretch;}`
Note	As of early 2018, there are plans to have this property apply to many (or all) elements, and be given the values `start` and `end` to replicate `flex-start` and `flex-end` behavior for non-flex environments.

all   Inh. N Anim. N

Values	`inherit` | `initial` | `unset`
Initial value	See individual properties
Computed value	As declared
Applies to	All elements
Description	Applies the declared value to all properties *except* `direction` and `unicode-bidi`, which are exempted for accessibility and historical reasons. This allows an author to, for example, force an element to reset all of its style properties to their default values, thus blocking the inheritance of values for all properties (except the exempted two).
Examples	`*.blendin {all: inherit;}` `*.embedded {all: unset;}`

animation   Inh. N Anim. N

Values	[*<animation-name>* ‖ *<animation-duration>* ‖ *<animation-timing-function>* ‖ *<animation-delay>* ‖ *<animation-iteration-count>* ‖ *<animation-direction>* ‖ *<animation-fill-mode>* ‖ *<animation-play-state>*]#
Initial value	`0s ease 0s 1 normal none running none`
Computed value	As declared

Applies to	All elements, ::before and ::after pseudo-elements
Description	A shorthand property encompassing all the aspects of one or more comma-separated CSS animations. The parts of the value can occur in any order. Therefore, beware possible ambiguity in the delay and duration values. As of this writing, it is most likely that the first time value will be taken to define the duration and the second to define the delay, but this cannot be guaranteed.
Examples	`div#slide {animation: 'slide' 2.5s linear 0 1 normal;}` `h1 {animation: 'bounce' 0.5s 0.33s ease-in-out infinite alternate;}`

animation-delay   Inh. N Anim. N

Values	*<time>#*
Initial value	0s
Computed value	As declared
Applies to	All elements, ::before and ::after pseudo-elements
Description	Defines the amount of time that the user agent waits before starting the CSS animation(s). The timer starts when the user agent applies the animation CSS. For a noninteractive element, this is likely (but not guaranteed) to be at the end of page load.
Examples	`body {animation-delay: 1s, 2000ms, 4s;}` `a:hover {animation-delay: 400ms;}`

animation-direction   Inh. N Anim. N

Values	[normal | reverse | alternate | alternate-reverse]#
Initial value	normal
Computed value	As declared

Applies to	All elements, `::before` and `::after` pseudo-elements
Description	Specifies whether a CSS animation with more than one cycle (see `animation-iteration-count`) should always go the same direction or should reverse direction on every other cycle. For example, an `alternate` animation that moves an element 300 pixels to the right would move it 300 pixels to the left on every other cycle, thus returning it to its starting position. Setting that same animation to `normal` would cause the element to move 300 pixels right, then jump back to its starting place and move 300 pixels right again, over and over until the animation stops (assuming it ever does).
| Examples | ```
body {animation-direction:
    alternate, normal, normal;}
#scanner {animation-direction: normal;}
``` |

animation-duration   Inh. N   Anim. N

Values	*<time>*#
Initial value	0s
Computed value	As declared
Applies to	All elements, `::before` and `::after` pseudo-elements
Description	Defines the length of time it should take for each cycle of a CSS animation to run from start to finish. Therefore, in animations with only one cycle, it defines the total time of the animation. The default value, 0s, means that there will be no animation besides moving the element from its start state to its end state. Negative values are converted to 0s.
| Examples | ```
h1 {animation-duration: 10s, 5s, 2.5s, 1250ms;}
.zip {animation-duration: 90ms;}
``` |

animation-iteration-count

Values   [<*number*> | infinite]#

Initial value   1

Computed value As declared

Applies to   All elements, ::before and ::after pseudo-elements

Description   Defines the number of cycles in the animation(s). The default value, 1, means that the animation will run exactly once, going from the start state to the end state. A fractional value (e.g., 2.75) means the animation will be halted midway through its final cycle. A value of 0 means that there will be no animation; negative values are converted to 0. As its name implies, infinite means the animation will never end. Use with caution.

Examples   body {animation-iteration-count: 2, 1, 7.5875;}
                      ol.dance {animation-iteration-count: infinite;}

animation-name

Values   [<*single-animation-name*> | none]#

Initial value   none

Computed value As declared

Applies to   All elements, ::before and ::after pseudo-elements

Description   Defines the declared name(s) of CSS animation(s). Each name refers to a CSS animation keyframe at-rule. If no animation name is declared or the keyword none is supplied, the animation is not run regardless of the values of any other animation properties. For example, given animation-name: bounce, none, jumper and that the animation name jumper has not been defined, the first animation will run but the second and third will not.

Examples   html {animation-name: turn, slide, none;}
         h2 {animation-name: flip;}

---

animation-play-state   Inh. N Anim. N

Values   [running | paused]#

Initial value   running

Computed value   As declared

Applies to   All elements, ::before and ::after pseudo-elements

Description   Defines the run state of one or more CSS animations. The default state of running is the most useful in static CSS environments, but it can be used to easily stop or start animations via DOM scripting or interactive CSS (e.g., :hover).

Examples   pre {animation-play-state:
                 running, paused, running;}
             table {animation-play-state: running;}

---

animation-timing-function   Inh. N Anim. N

Values   [ease | linear | ease-in | ease-out | ease-in-out |
             step-start | step-end | steps(*<integer>*, start) |
             steps(*<integer>*, end) | cubic-bezier(*<number>*,
             <number>,*<number>*,*<number>*)]#

Initial value   ease

Computed value   As declared

Applies to   All elements, ::before and ::after pseudo-elements

Description   Defines how an animation is run over the course of the animation's full cycle or within an individual keyframe, depending on where the property is used. The keywords are all defined to have cubic-bezier() equivalents; for example, linear is equivalent to cubic-bezier(0,0,1,1). They should therefore have consistent effects across user agents

—but, as always, authors are cautioned not to count on that.

Examples
```
h1 {animation-timing-function: ease, ease-in,
    cubic-bezier(0.13,0.42,0.67,0.75)}
p {animation-timing-function: linear;}
```

---

backface-visibility   Inh. N Anim. N

Values	visible | hidden
Initial value	visible
Computed value	As declared
Applies to	Any transformable element
Description	Defines whether the back side of an element is visible once the element has been rotated in a simulated 3D space and is "facing away" from the viewer. If the value is hidden, the element will be effectively invisible until it is rotated such that the front side of the element is once more "facing toward" the viewer.
Examples	div.card {backface-visibility: hidden;} span.cubeside {backface-visibility: visible;}

---

background   Inh. N Anim. P

Values	[*<bg-layer>* ,]* *<final-bg-layer>*
Initial value	Refer to individual properties
Computed value	Refer to individual properties
Applies to	All elements
Animatable	Refer to individual background properties to see which are animatable
Description	A shorthand way of expressing the various background properties of one or more element backgrounds using a single declaration. As with all shorthands, this property will set all of the allowed values (e.g., the repeat, position, and so on) to their defaults if the values are not explicitly supplied.

Thus, the following two rules will have the same appearance:

```
background: yellow;
background: yellow none top left repeat;
```

Furthermore, these defaults can override previous declarations made with more specific background properties. For example, given the following rules:

```
h1 {background-repeat: repeat-x;}
h1, h2 {background: yellow url(headback.gif);}
```

the repeat value for both h1 and h2 elements will be set to the default of repeat, overriding the previously declared value of repeat-x.

When declaring multiple backgrounds, only the last may have a background color. In cases where multiple background images overlap, the images are stacked with the first highest and the last lowest. This is the exact reverse of how overlapping is handled in CSS positioning, and so may seem counterintuitive.

Examples
```
body {background: white url(bg41.gif)
    fixed center repeat-x;}
p {background:
    url(/pix/water.png) center repeat-x,
    top left url(/pix/stone.png) #555;}
pre {background: yellow;}
```

background-attachment   Inh. N Anim. N

Values	[scroll | fixed | local]#
Initial value	scroll
Computed value	As declared
Applies to	All elements
Description	Defines whether background images scroll along with the element when the document is scrolled. This property can be used to create "aligned" backgrounds; for more details, see Chapter 9 of *CSS: The Definitive Guide*, 4th Edition.

Examples	`body {background-attachment:`
	`    scroll, scroll, fixed;}`
	`div.fixbg {background-attachment: fixed;}`

background-blend-mode   Inh. N Anim. N

Values	[normal | multiply | screen | overlay | darken | lighten | color-dodge | color-burn | hard-light | soft-light | difference | exclusion | hue | saturation | color | luminosity]#
Initial value	normal
Computed value	As declared
Applies to	All elements
Description	Changes how overlapping background images are composited against an "empty" backdrop. The "backdrop" here is a transparent layer underneath the background color. The default of normal imposes simple alpha blending, as CSS has permitted since its inception. The others cause the background image and its backdrop to be combined in various ways; for example, lighten means that the final result will show, at each pixel, either the image or its backdrop, whichever is lighter. darken is the same, except the darker of the two pixels will be shown. The results of these are likely to be familiar to users of Photoshop or any other graphic-editing tool. Compositing of multiple background layers is done back to front.

Examples	`li.shadowed {background-blend-mode: darken;}`
	`aside {background-blend-mode:`
	`    color-burn, luminosity, darken;}`

background-clip   Inh. N Anim. N

Values	[border-box | padding-box | content-box | text]#
Initial value	border-box
Computed value	As declared

Applies to	All elements
Description	Defines the boundary within the element box at which the background is clipped (that is, no longer drawn). Historically, this has been equivalent to the default value of border-box, where the background goes to the outer edge of the border area. This property allows more constrained clipping boxes at the outer edge of the padding area and at the content edge itself.
Examples	body {background-clip: content-box;} .callout {background-clip: content-box, border-box, padding-box;}

background-color   Inh. N   Anim. Y

Values	<color>
Initial value	transparent
Computed value	As declared
Applies to	All elements
Description	Defines a solid color for the background of the element. This color fills the box defined by the value of background-clip—by default, the content, padding, and border areas of the element, extending to the outer edge of the element's border. Borders that have transparent sections (such as dashed borders) will show the background color through the transparent sections in cases where the background color extends into the border area.
Examples	h4 {background-color: white;} p {background-color: rgba(50%,50%,50%,0.33);} pre {background-color: #FF9;}

background-image   Inh. N   Anim. N

Values	[<image> | none]#
Initial value	none
Computed value	As declared, but with all URIs made absolute

Applies to	All elements
Description	Places one or more images in the background of the element. Depending on the value of background-repeat, the image may tile infinitely, along one axis, or not at all. The initial background image (the origin image) is placed according to the value of background-position.

Examples	`body {background-image:`
	`    url(bg41.gif), url(bg43.png), url(bg51.jpg);}`
	`h2 {background-image:`
	`    url(http://www.pix.org/dots.png);}`

background-origin   Inh. N Anim. N

Values	[border-box | padding-box | content-box]#
Initial value	padding-box
Computed value	As declared
Applies to	All elements
Description	Defines the boundary within the element box against which background image positioning is calculated. Historically, this has been equivalent to the default value of padding-box. This property allows for different positioning contexts. Note that if the value of background-origin is "further out" than the value for background-clip, and the image is positioned to an edge, part of it may be clipped. For example:

```
div#example {background-origin: border-box;
    background-clip: content-box;
    background-position: 100% 100%;}
```

In this case the image will be placed so that its bottom-right corner aligns with the bottom-right corner of the outer border edge, but the only parts of it that will be visible are those that fall within the content area.

Examples	`html, body {background-origin: border-box;}` `h1 {background-origin: content-box, padding-box;}`

background-position   Inh. N Anim. Y

Values	*<position>#*
Initial value	0% 0%
Computed value	The absolute length offsets, if *<length>* is specified; otherwise, percentage values
Percentages	Refer to the corresponding point on both the element and the origin image
Applies to	Block-level and replaced elements
Description	Defines the position(s) of one or more backgrounds' origin images (as defined by background-image); this is the point from which any background repetition or tiling will occur. Percentage values define not only a point within the element, but also the same point in the origin image itself. That means (for example) an image can be centered by declaring its position to be 50% 50%. When percentage or length values are used, the first is always the horizontal position and the second is the vertical position. If only one value is given, it sets the horizontal position, while the missing value is assumed to be either center or 50%. Negative values are permitted and may place the origin image outside the element's content area without actually rendering it. The context within which an origin image is placed can be affected by the value of background-origin.
Examples	body {background-position: top center;} div#navbar {background-position: right, 50% 75%, 0 40px;} pre {background-position: 10px 50%;}

background-repeat   Inh. N Anim. N

Values	*<repeat-style>#*
Definition	
<repeat-style>	repeat-x	repeat-y	[repeat	space	round	no-repeat]{1,2}

Initial value	repeat
Computed value	As declared
Applies to	All elements
Description	Defines the tiling pattern for one or more background images. The repetition begins from the origin image, which is defined as the value of background-image and is placed according to the value of background-position (and possibly background-origin). For the keywords space and round, the image is tiled as many times as it will fit in the background area without being clipped, and then the first and last images are placed against their respective background edges. The difference is that space causes the intervening images to be regularly spaced, and round causes them to be stretched to touch each other. Note that repeat-x is equivalent to repeat no-repeat, and repeat-y is equivalent to no-repeat repeat.

Examples	`body {background-repeat: no-repeat;}`
	`h2 {background-repeat: repeat-x, repeat-y;}`
	`ul {background-repeat:`
	`   repeat-y, round space, repeat;}`

background-size   Inh. N Anim. Y

Values	[[<length>	<percentage>	auto]{1,2}	cover	contain]#
Initial value	auto
Computed value	As declared, but with all lengths made absolute and any missing auto keywords added
Applies to	All elements
Description	Defines the size of one or more background origin images. If two keywords are used (e.g., 50px 25%), the first defines the horizontal size of the image and the second defines the vertical size. The origin image can be deformed to exactly cover the background with 100% 100%. By contrast, cover scales

---

up the image to cover the entire background even if some of it exceeds the background area and is thus clipped, and `contain` scales up the origin image so that at least one of its dimensions exactly fills the corresponding axis of the background area.

Examples
```
body {background-size: 100% 90%;}
div.photo {background-size: cover;}
```

---

border   Inh. N Anim. P

Values	[*<border-width>* ‖ *<border-style>* ‖ *<border-color>*]
Initial value	Refer to individual properties
Computed value	As declared
Applies to	All elements
Animatable	Border width and color; not border style
Description	A shorthand property that defines the width, color, and style of an element's border. Note that while none of the values are actually required, omitting a border style will result in no border being applied because the default border style is none.

Examples	`h1 {border: 2px dashed olive;}`
	`a:link {border: blue solid 1px;}`
	`p.warning {border: double 5px red;}`

---

border-bottom   Inh. N Anim. P

Values	[*<border-width>* ‖ *<border-style>* ‖ *<border-color>*]
Initial value	See individual properties
Computed value	See individual properties (`border-width`, etc.)
Applies to	All elements
Animatable	Border width and color; not border style
Description	A shorthand property that defines the width, color, and style of the bottom border of an element. As

with border, omission of a border style will result in no border appearing.

Examples
```
ul {border-bottom: 0.5in groove green;}
a:active {border-bottom: purple 2px dashed;}
```

border-bottom-color   Inh. N   Anim. Y

Values	*<color>*
Initial value	currentColor
Computed value	A color
Applies to	All elements
Description	Defines the color for the visible portions of the bottom border of an element. The border's style must be something other than none or hidden for any visible border to appear.
Examples	`ul {border-bottom-color: green;}` `a:active {border-bottom-color: purple;}`

border-bottom-left-radius   Inh. N   Anim. Y

Values	[*<length>* | *<percentage>*]{1,2}
Initial value	0
Computed value	Two values, each a *<percentage>* or *<length>* made absolute
Percentages	Calculated with respect to the relevant dimension of the border box
Applies to	All elements, except internal table elements
Description	Defines the rounding radius for the bottom-left corner of an element's border. If two values are supplied, the first is the horizontal radius and the second is the vertical radius. See border-radius for a description of how the values create the rounding shape.
Examples	`h1 {border-bottom-left-radius: 10%;}` `h2 {border-bottom-left-radius: 1em 10px;}`

border-bottom-right-radius   Inh. N   Anim. Y

Values	[*<length>* | *<percentage>*]{1,2}
Initial value	0
Computed value	Two values, each a *<percentage>* or *<length>* made absolute
Percentages	Calculated with respect to the relevant dimension of the border box
Applies to	All elements, except internal table elements
Description	Defines the rounding radius for the bottom-right corner of an element's border. If two values are supplied, the first is the horizontal radius and the second is the vertical radius. See border-radius for a description of how the values create the rounding shape.
Examples	h1 {border-bottom-right-radius: 10%;} h2 {border-bottom-right-radius: 1em 10px;}

border-bottom-style   Inh. N   Anim. N

Values	none | hidden | dotted | dashed | solid | double | groove | ridge | inset | outset
Initial value	none
Computed value	As declared
Applies to	All elements
Description	Defines the style for the bottom border of an element. The value must be something other than none or hidden for any border to appear.
Examples	ul {border-bottom-style: groove;} a:active {border-bottom-style: dashed;}

border-bottom-width   Inh. N   Anim. Y

Values	[thin | medium | thick | *<length>*]

Initial value	See individual properties
Computed value	See individual properties (border-top-style, etc.)
Applies to	All elements
Description	Defines the width for the bottom border of an element, which will take effect only if the border's style is something other than none or hidden. If the border style is none, the border width is effectively reset to 0. Negative length values are not permitted.
Examples	ul {border-bottom-width: 0.5in;} a:active {border-bottom-width: 2px;}

border-collapse   Inh. Y Anim. Y

Values	collapse	separate	inherit
Initial value	separate
Computed value	As declared
Applies to	Elements with the display value table or table-inline
Description	Defines the layout model used in laying out the borders in a table—i.e., those applied to cells, rows, and so forth. Although the property applies only to tables, it is inherited by all the elements within the table and actually used by them.
Example	table {border-collapse: separate; border-spacing: 3px 5px;}
Note	In CSS2, the default was collapse.

border-color   Inh. N Anim. Y

Values	<color>{1,4}
Initial value	See individual properties
Computed value	See individual properties (border-top-color, etc.)
Applies to	All elements

Description	A shorthand property that sets the color for the visible portions of the overall border of an element or sets a different color for each of the four sides. Remember that a border's style must be something other than `none` or `hidden` for any visible border to appear.
Examples	`h1 {border-color: purple;}` `a:visited {border-color: maroon;}`

---

border-image
Inh. N Anim. P

Values	*<border-image-source>* ‖ *<border-image-slice>* [/ *<border-image-width>*	/ *<border-image-width>*? / *<border-image-outset>*]? ‖ *<border-image-repeat>*
Initial value	See individual properties
Computed value	See individual properties
Applies to	See individual properties
Animatable	Refer to individual border-image properties to see which are animatable
Description	A shorthand property that defines the source, slicing pattern, border width, degree of extension, and repetition of an image-based border. The syntax is somewhat unusual compared to the rest of CSS, so take extra time with it. For example, three of the five values possible are slash-separated and must be listed in a specific order.
	Note that it is effectively impossible to take a simple image (say, a star) and repeat it around the edges of an element. To create that effect, you must create a single image that contains nine copies of the image you wish to repeat in a 3×3 grid. It may also be necessary to set `border-width` (*not* `border-image-width`) to be large enough to show the image, depending on the value of `border-image-outset`.
Examples	`div.starry {border-image:` `  url(stargrid.png) 5px repeat;}`

```
aside {border-image: url(asides.png)
    100 50 150 / 8 3 13 / 2 stretch round;}
```

border-image-outset   Inh. N Anim. Y

Values	[<length>	<number>]{1,4}
Initial value	0
Computed value	Four values, each a number or <length> made absolute
Applies to	All elements, except internal table elements when border-collapse is collapse
Description	Defines the distance by which a border image may exceed the border area of the element. The values define distances from the top, right, bottom, and left edges of the border image, in that order. Numbers are calculated with respect to the image's intrinsic coordinate system; thus, for a raster image, the number 7 is taken to mean seven pixels. Images in formats such as SVG may have different coordinate systems. Negative values are not permitted.
Examples	aside {border-image-outset: 2;} div#pow {border-image-outset: 10 17 13 5;}

border-image-repeat   Inh. N Anim. N

Values	[stretch	repeat	round	space]{1,2}
Initial value	stretch
Computed value	Two keywords, one for each axis
Applies to	All elements, except internal table elements when border-collapse is collapse
Description	Defines the repetition pattern (or lack thereof) of the sides of a border image. stretch causes a single copy of the image to be stretched to fit the border segment (top, right, bottom, or left). repeat "tiles" the image in a manner familiar from background images, though border images are only ever tiled

along one axis. round "tiles" the border image as many times as it will fit without clipping, then (if necessary) scales the entire set of tiled images to exactly fit the border segment.

Examples
```
div.starry {border-image-repeat: repeat;}
aside {border-image-repeat: stretch round;}
```

---

border-image-slice   Inh. N Anim. P

Values   [*<number>* | *<percentage>*]{1,4} && fill?

Initial value   100%

Computed value   Four values, each a number or percentage, and optionally the fill keyword

Percentages   Refer to the size of the border image

Applies to   All elements, except internal table elements when border-collapse is collapse

Animatable   *<number>* and *<percentage>* values only

Description   Defines "slice distances," which are offsets from the top, right, bottom, and left edges of the border image. Taken together, they divide the image into nine regions, which correspond to the eight segments of the element's border (four corners and four sides) and the element's background area.

In cases where two opposite regions combine to exceed the total of the dimension they share, both are made completely transparent. For example, if the top slice offset value is 10 and the bottom slice offset value is 20, but the source image is only 25 pixels tall, the two exceed the height of the image. Thus, both the top and bottom segments of the border will be entirely transparent. The same holds for right and left slices and width. Corners are never forcibly made transparent, even in cases where their slices may overlap in the source image.

Examples
```
div.starry {border-image-slice: 5px;}
aside {border-image-slice: 100 50 150;}
```

---

border-image-source

Inh. N   Anim. N

Values	none | *<image>*
Initial value	none
Computed value	none, or the image with its URI made absolute
Applies to	All elements, except internal table elements when `border-collapse` is `collapse`
Description	Supplies the location of the image to be used as an element's border image.

Examples	`div.starry {border-image-source:`
	`    url(stargrid.png);}`
	`aside {border-image-source: url(asides.png);}`

border-image-width

Inh. N   Anim. Y

Values	[*<length>* | *<percentage>* | *<number>* | auto]{1,4}
Initial value	1
Computed value	Four values, each a percentage, a number, a *<length>* made absolute, or the auto keyword
Percentages	Relative to the width/height of the entire border image area; that is, the outer edges of the border box
Applies to	All elements, except table elements when `border-collapse` is `collapse`
Description	Defines an image width for each of the four sides of an image border. Border image slices that have a different width than the border image width value are scaled to match it, which may impact how they are repeated. For example, if the right edge of an image border is 10 pixels wide, but `border-image-width: 3px` has been declared, the border images along the right side are scaled to be three pixels wide.

Note that `border-image-width` is different from `border-width`: a border image's width can be different than the width of the border area. In cases where the image is wider or taller than the border area, it |

96 | Chapter 4: Property Reference

will be clipped by default (but `border-image-outset` may prevent this). If it is narrower or shorter than the border area, it will not be scaled up. Negative values are not permitted.

Examples
```
aside {border-image-width: 8 3 13;}
div#pow{border-image-width: 25px 35;}
```

border-left   Inh. N Anim. P

Values	[*<border-width>* ‖ *<border-style>* ‖ *<border-color>*]
Initial value	See individual properties
Computed value	See individual properties (`border-width`, etc.)
Applies to	All elements
Animatable	Border width and color; not border style
Description	A shorthand property that defines the width, color, and style of the left border of an element. As with `border`, omission of a border style will result in no border appearing.
Examples	`p {border-left: 3em solid gray;}` `pre {border-left: double black 4px;}`

border-left-color   Inh. N Anim. Y

Values	*<color>*
Initial value	currentColor
Computed value	A color
Applies to	All elements
Description	Defines the color for the visible portions of the left border of an element. The border's style must be something other than none or hidden for any visible border to appear.
Examples	`p {border-left-color: gray;}` `pre {border-left-color: black;}`

border-left-style

Values	none | hidden | dotted | dashed | solid | double | groove | ridge | inset | outset
Initial value	none
Computed value	As declared
Applies to	All elements
Description	Defines the style for the left border of an element. The value must be something other than none or hidden for any border to appear.
Examples	p {border-left-style: solid;} pre {border-left-style: double;}

border-left-width

Values	thin | medium | thick | <length>
Initial value	medium
Computed value	An absolute length, or 0 if the style of the border is none or hidden; otherwise, as declared
Applies to	All elements
Description	Defines the width for the left border of an element, which will take effect only if the border's style is something other than none or hidden. If the border style is none, the border width is effectively reset to 0. Negative length values are not permitted.
Examples	p {border-left-width: 3em;} pre {border-left-width: 4px;}

border-radius

Values	[<length> | <percentage>]{1,4} [/ [<length> | <percentage>]{1,4}]?
Initial value	0

Computed value	Four values, each a *<percentage>* or *<length>* made absolute
Percentages	Calculated with respect to the relevant dimension of the border box
Applies to	All elements, except internal table elements
Description	A shorthand property that defines the rounding radius for the bottom-right corner of an element's border. The actual corners will be the height and width declared. Thus, given:

```
.callout {border-radius: 10px;}
```

each corner of an element with a class of callout will have a rounding that is 10 pixels across, as measured from the beginning of the rounding to the outer side edge of the element, and is similarly 10 pixels high. This can be visualized as if the element had 10-pixel-radius (20-pixel-diameter) circles drawn in its corners, and then the border were bent along the circles' edges.

Using fewer than four values causes the supplied values to be repeated in the familiar pattern (see margin, padding, etc.), but with a slight offset. Rather than being Top-Right-Bottom-Left (TRBL, or "trouble"), the pattern is TopLeft-TopRight-BottomRight-BottomLeft (TLTRBRBL, or "tilter burble"). Otherwise, the repeat pattern is the same.

Percentages, when used, are calculated with respect to the size of the element's border box (the box defined by the outer edges of the element's border area) dimension on the related axis.

Examples	

```
a[href] {border-radius: 0.5em 50%;}
.callout {border-radius:
   10px 20px 30px 40px /
   1em 2em 3em 4em;}
```

border-right   Inh. N   Anim. P

Values	[*<border-width>* ‖ *<border-style>* ‖ *<border-color>*]
Initial value	See individual properties
Computed value	See individual properties (border-width, etc.)
Applies to	All elements
Animatable	Border width and color; not border style
Description	A shorthand property that defines the width, color, and style of the right border of an element. As with border, omission of a border style will result in no border appearing.
Examples	img {border-right: 30px dotted blue;} h3 {border-right: cyan 1em inset;}

border-right-color   Inh. N   Anim. Y

Values	*<color>*
Initial value	currentColor
Computed value	A color
Applies to	All elements
Description	Defines the color for the visible portions of the right border of an element. The border's style must be something other than none or hidden for any visible border to appear.
Examples	img {border-right-color: blue;} h3 {border-right-color: cyan;}

border-right-style   Inh. N   Anim. N

Values	none | hidden | dotted | dashed | solid | double | groove | ridge | inset | outset
Initial value	none
Computed value	As declared

Applies to	All elements
Description	Defines the style for the right border of an element. The value must be something other than none or hidden for any border to appear.
Examples	img {border-right-style: dotted;} h3 {border-right-style: inset;}

border-right-width   Inh. N Anim. Y

Values	thin | medium | thick | <length>
Initial value	medium
Computed value	An absolute length, or 0 if the style of the border is none or hidden; otherwise, as declared
Applies to	All elements
Description	Defines the width for the right border of an element, which will take effect only if the border's style is something other than none or hidden. If the border style is none, the border width is effectively reset to 0. Negative length values are not permitted.
Examples	img {border-right-width: 30px;} h3 {border-right-width: 1em;}

border-spacing   Inh. Y Anim. Y

Values	<length> <length>?
Initial value	0
Computed value	Two absolute lengths
Applies to	Elements with the display value table or table-inline
Description	Defines the distance between table cell borders in the separated borders table layout model. The first of the two length values is the horizontal separation and the second is the vertical separation. Although the property applies only to tables, it is inherited by all of the elements within the table.

Examples	```table {border-spacing: 0;}``` ```table {border-spacing: 3px 5px;}```
Note	This property is ignored unless the value of border-collapse is separate.

border-style   Inh. N Anim. N

Values	[none | hidden | solid | dotted | dashed | double | groove | ridge | inset | outset]{1,4}
Initial value	See individual properties
Computed value	See individual properties (border-top-style, etc.)
Applies to	All elements
Description	A shorthand property used to define the styles for the overall border of an element or for each side individually. The value of any border must be something other than none or hidden for the border to appear. Note that setting border-style to none (its default value) will result in no border at all. In such a case, any value of border-width will be ignored and the width of the border will be set to 0. Any unrecognized value from the list of values should be reinterpreted as solid.
Examples	```h1 {border-style: solid;}``` ```img {border-style: inset;}```

border-top   Inh. N Anim. P

Values	[*<border-width>* || *<border-style>* || *<border-color>*]
Initial value	See individual properties
Computed value	See individual properties (border-width, etc.)
Applies to	All elements
Animatable	Border width and color; not border style
Description	A shorthand property that defines the width, color, and style of the top border of an element. As with

border, omission of a border style will result in no
border appearing.

Examples
```
ul {border-top: 0.5in solid black;}
h1 {border-top: dashed 1px gray;}
```

border-top-color   Inh. N   Anim. Y

Values   *<color>*

Initial value   currentColor

Computed value   A color

Applies to   All elements

Description   Sets the color for the visible portions of the top bor-
                     der of an element. The border's style must be some-
                     thing other than none or hidden for any visible bor-
                     der to appear.

Examples
```
ul {border-top-color: black;}
h1 {border-top-color: gray;}
```

border-top-left-radius   Inh. N   Anim. Y

Values   [*<length>* | *<percentage>*]{1,2}

Initial value   0

Computed value   Two values, each a *<percentage>* or *<length>* made
                     absolute

Percentages   Calculated with respect to the relevant dimension of
                     the border box

Applies to   All elements, except internal table elements

Description   Defines the rounding radius for the top-left corner
                     of an element's border. If two values are supplied,
                     the first is the horizontal radius and the second is
                     the vertical radius. See border-radius for a descrip-
                     tion of how the values create the rounding shape.

Examples
```
h1 {border-top-left-radius: 10%;}
h2 {border-top-left-radius: 1em 10px;}
```

border-top-right-radius   Inh. N Anim. Y

Values	[*<length>* | *<percentage>*]{1,2}
Initial value	0
Computed value	Two values, each a *<percentage>* or *<length>* made absolute
Percentages	Calculated with respect to the relevant dimension of the border box
Applies to	All elements, except internal table elements
Description	Defines the rounding radius for the top-right corner of an element's border. If two values are supplied, the first is the horizontal radius and the second is the vertical radius. See border-radius for a description of how the values create the rounding shape.
Examples	h1 {border-top-right-radius: 10%;} h2 {border-top-right-radius: 1em 10px;}

border-top-style   Inh. N Anim. N

Values	none | hidden | dotted | dashed | solid | double | groove | ridge | inset | outset
Initial value	none
Computed value	As declared
Applies to	All elements
Description	Defines the style for the top border of an element. The value must be something other than none or hidden for any border to appear.
Examples	ul {border-top-style: solid;} h1 {border-top-style: dashed;}

border-top-width   Inh. N Anim. Y

Values	thin | medium | thick | *<length>*
Initial value	medium

Computed value	An absolute length, or 0 if the style of the border is `none` or `hidden`; otherwise, as declared
Applies to	All elements
Description	Defines the width for the top border of an element, which will take effect only if the border's style is something other than `none` or `hidden`. If the style is `none`, the width is effectively reset to 0. Negative length values are not permitted.
Examples	`ul {border-top-width: 0.5in;}` `h1 {border-top-width: 1px;}`

border-width   Inh. N   Anim. Y

Values	[`thin` | `medium` | `thick` | *<length>*]{1,4}
Initial value	See individual properties
Computed value	See individual properties (`border-top-style`, etc.)
Applies to	All elements
Description	A shorthand property that defines the width for the overall border of an element or for each side individually. The width will take effect for a given border only if the border's style is something other than `none` or `hidden`. If the border style is `none`, the border width is effectively reset to 0. Negative length values are not permitted.
Examples	`h1 {border-width: 2ex;}` `img {border-width: 5px thick thin 1em;}`

bottom   Inh. N   Anim. P

Values	*<length>* | *<percentage>* | `auto`
Initial value	`auto`
Computed value	For static elements, `auto`; for length values, the corresponding absolute length; for percentage values, the specified value; otherwise, `auto`
Percentages	Refer to the height of the containing block

Applies to	Positioned elements
Animatable	*<length>* and *<percentage>* values only
Description	Defines the offset between the bottom outer margin edge of a positioned element and the bottom edge of its containing block. For relatively positioned elements, if both bottom and top are auto, their computed values are both 0; if one of them is auto, it becomes the negative of the other; if neither is auto, bottom will become the negative of the value of top.
| **Examples** | ```
div#footer {position: fixed; bottom: 0;}
sup {position: relative; bottom: 0.5em;
    vertical-align: baseline;}
``` |

box-decoration-break   Inh. N Anim. N

Values	slice | clone
Initial value	slice
Computed value	As declared
Applies to	All elements
Description	Defines whether the decorations—the background, padding, borders, rounded corners, border image, and box shadow—of a box that has been rendered in multiple pieces are applied to each piece separately or applied to the entire box before it is broken apart.
	The most common case is an inline element that wraps across one or more line breaks. With the default behavior, slice, the pieces of the inline element are drawn as though the whole element was laid out in a single line and then sliced apart at each line break. If clone is declared, then each piece of the element is decorated as though they were separate elements sharing the same styles.
	box-decoration-break also applies to block boxes that are split across columns or pages.
| **Examples** | ```
span {box-decoration-break: clone;}
a {box-decoration-break: slice;}
``` |

box-shadow

Values	none | [inset? && <*length*>{2,4} && <*color*>?]#
Initial value	none
Computed value	<*length*> values as absolute length values; <*color*> values as computed internally; otherwise, as declared
Applies to	All elements
Description	Defines one or more shadows that are derived from the shape of the element box. Either outset ("drop") shadows or inset shadows can be defined, the latter with use of the optional `inset` keyword. Without that keyword, the shadow will be outset.
	The four length values that can be declared are, in order: horizontal offset, vertical offset, blur distance, and spread distance. When positive, the offset values go down and to the right; when negative, they go back and to the left. Positive spread values increase the size of the shadow and negative values contract it. Blur values cannot be negative.
	Note that all shadows are clipped by the element's border edge. Thus, an outset shadow is only drawn outside the border edge. A semitransparent or fully transparent element background will *not* reveal an outset shadow "behind" the element. Similarly, inset shadows are only visible inside the border edge and are never drawn beyond it.
| **Examples** | ```
h1 {box-shadow: 5px 10px gray;}
table th {box-shadow:
    inset 0.5em 0.75em 5px −2px
    rgba(255,0,0,0.5);}
``` |

box-sizing

Values	content-box | padding-box | border-box
Initial value	content-box
```

Computed value	As declared
Applies to	All elements that accept `width` or `height` values
Description	Defines whether the `height` and `width` of the element define the dimensions of the content box (the historical behavior) or the border box. If the latter, the value of `width` defines the distance from the left outer border edge to the right outer border edge; similarly, `height` defines the distance from the top outer border edge to the bottom outer border edge. Any padding or border widths are "subtracted" from those dimensions instead of the historical "additive" behavior. Thus, given:

```
body {box-sizing: border-box;
   width: 880px; padding: 0 20px;}
```

the final width of the content area will be 840 pixels (880–20–20). |
| **Example** | `body {box-sizing: padding-box;}` |

caption-side   Inh. Y   Anim. N

Values	top | bottom
Initial value	top
Computed value	As declared
Applies to	Elements with the `display` value `table-caption`
Description	Defines the placement of a table caption with respect to the table box. The caption is rendered as though it were a block-level element placed just before (or after) the table.
Example	`caption {caption-side: top;}`
Note	The values `left` and `right` appeared in CSS2 but were later dropped due to a lack of widespread support.

clear

Inh. N   Anim. N

Values	left | right | both | none
Initial value	none
Computed value	As declared
Applies to	Block-level elements
Description	Defines to which side (or sides) of an element no floating element may be placed. If normal layout of a cleared element would result in a floated element appearing on the cleared side, the cleared element is pushed down until it sits below (clears) the floated element. In CSS1 and CSS2, this is accomplished by automatically increasing the top margin of the cleared element. In CSS2.1, clearance space is added above the element's top margin, but the margin itself is not altered. In either case, the end result is that the element's top outer border edge is just below the bottom outer margin edge of a floated element on the declared side.
Examples	h1 {clear: both;} p + h3 {clear: right;}

clip-path

Inh. N   Anim. P

Values	none | <uri> | [[inset() | circle() | ellipse() | polygon()] ‖ [border-box | padding-box | content-box | margin-box | fill-box | stroke-box | view-box]]
Initial value	none
Computed value	As declared
Applies to	All elements (in SVG, applies to all graphics elements and all container elements except the defs element)
Animatable	inset(), circle(), ellipse(), and polygon() values

Description	Defines a clipping shape inside of which an element is visible, and outside of which it is invisible. url() values can be used to refer to an SVG file or an SVG clipPath element to be used as the clipping shape.

Examples	`p.clipped {clip-path: url(shapes.svg#cloud02);}`
	`p.rounded {clip-path:`
	`    ellipse(100px 50px at 75% 25%);}`
	`p.diamond {clip-path:`
	`    polygon(50% 0, 100% 50%, 50% 100%, 0 50%);}`

clip-rule   Inh. N Anim. N

Values	nonzero | evenodd
Initial value	nonzero
Computed value	As declared
Applies to	All SVG graphics elements (circle, ellipse, image, line, path, polygon, polyline, rect, text, and use) *if and only if* they are children of a clipPath element
Description	Alters the way in which portions of a path that overlap each other cause the resulting shape to be filled. A nonzero rule causes the entire shape to be filled. evenodd can result in portions of the shape's interior being fully transparent.
Examples	`span.fullshape {clip-rule: nonzero;}` `span.knockouts {clip-rule: evenodd;}`

color   Inh. Y Anim. Y

Values	*<color>*
Initial value	User agent–specific
Computed value	As declared
Applies to	All elements
Description	Defines the foreground color of an element, which in HTML rendering means the text of an element; raster images are not affected by color. This is also the color applied to any borders of the element,

unless overridden by `border-color` or one of the other border color properties (`border-top-color`, etc.).

For color keywords (such as `navy`) and RGB hex values (such as `#008800` or `#080`), the computed value is the `rgb()` equivalent. For `transparent`, the computed value is `rgba(0,0,0,0)`; for `currentColor`, the computed value is `inherit`. For all other values, the computed value is the same as the declared value.

Examples
```
strong {color: rgb(255,128,128);}
h3 {color: navy;}
p.warning {color: #ff0000;}
pre.pastoral {color: rgba(0%,100%,0%,0.33334);}
```

content   Inh. N Anim. N

Values   `normal | [ <string> | <uri> | <counter> | attr(<identifier>) | open-quote | close-quote | no-open-quote | no-close-quote ]+`

Initial value   `normal`

Computed value For `<uri>` values, an absolute URI; for attribute references, the resulting string; otherwise, as declared

Applies to   `::before` and `::after` pseudo-elements

Description   Defines the generated content placed before or after an element. By default, this is likely to be inline content, but the type of box the content creates can be defined using the property `display`.

Examples
```
p::before {content: "Paragraph...";}
a[href]::after {content: "(" attr(href) ")";
    font-size: smaller;}
```

counter-increment   Inh. N Anim. N

Values   `[ <identifier> <integer>? ]+ | none`

Initial value   User agent–dependent

Computed value	As declared
Applies to	All elements
Description	With this property, counters can be incremented (or decremented) by any value, positive or negative or 0. If no *<integer>* is supplied, it defaults to 1.
Examples	h1 {counter-increment: section;} *.backward li {counter-increment: counter -1;}

counter-reset   Inh. N   Anim. N

Values	[*<identifier>* *<integer>*?]+	none
Initial value	User agent–dependent
Computed value	As declared
Applies to	All elements
Description	With this property, counters can be reset (or set for the first time) to any value, positive or negative. If no *<integer>* is supplied, it defaults to 0.
Examples	h1 {counter-reset: section;} h2 {counter-reset: subsec 1;}

cursor   Inh. Y   Anim. N

Values	[*<uri>* [*<number>* *<number>*]?,]* [auto | default | none | context-menu | help | pointer | progress | wait | cell | crosshair | text | vertical-text | alias | copy | move | no-drop | not-allowed | e-resize | n-resize | ne-resize | nw-resize | s-resize | se-resize | sw-resize | w-resize | ew-resize | ns-resize | nesw-resize | nwse-resize | col-resize | row-resize | all-scroll]
Initial value	auto
Computed value	For *<uri>* values, given that a *<uri>* resolves to a supported file type, a single absolute URI with optional *x,y* coordinates; otherwise, as declared

Applies to	All elements
Description	Defines the cursor shape to be used when a mouse pointer is placed within the boundary of an element. Authors are cautioned to remember that users are typically very aware of cursor changes and can be easily confused by changes that seem counterintuitive. For example, making any noninteractive element switch the cursor state to `pointer` is quite likely to cause user frustration.
	Note that the value syntax makes URI values optional, but the keyword mandatory. Thus, you can specify any number of URIs to external cursor resources, but the value *must* end with a keyword. Leaving off the keyword will cause conforming user agents to drop the declaration entirely.
	CSS3 allows two numbers to be supplied with a *<uri>* value. These define the *x,y* coordinates of the cursor's "active point"; that is, the point in the cursor that is used for determining hover states, active actions, and so forth. If no numbers are supplied and the cursor image has no "intrinsic hotspot" (to quote the specification), the top-left corner of the image is used (equivalent to 0 0). Note that the numbers are unitless and are interpreted relative to the "cursor's coordinate system" (to quote again).
Examples	`a.moreinfo {cursor: help;}` `a[href].external {cursor: url(globe.png), auto;}`

direction   Inh. Y Anim. Y

Values	ltr | rtl
Initial value	ltr
Computed value	As declared
Applies to	All elements
Description	Defines the base writing direction of blocks and the direction of embeddings and overrides for the Unicode Bidirectional Algorithm (sometimes called

bidi). Furthermore, it changes the way a number of properties and layout decisions are handled, including but not limited to the placement of table cells in a table row and the layout algorithms for block boxes.

For a variety of reasons, authors are strongly encouraged to use the HTML attribute dir rather than the CSS property direction. User agents that do not support bidirectional text are permitted to ignore this property.

Examples   `*:lang(en) {direction: ltr;}`
                  `*:lang(ar) {direction: rtl;}`

---

display   Inh. N Anim. N

Values   [*<display-outside>* || *<display-inside>*] | *<display-listitem>* | *<display-internal>* | *<display-box>* | *<display-legacy>*

Definitions

<display-outside> block | inline | run-in

<display-inside> flow | flow-root | table | flex | grid | ruby

<display-listitem> list-item && *<display-outside>*? && [flow | flow-root]?

<display-internal> table-row-group | table-header-group | table-footer-group | table-row | table-cell | table-column-group | table-column | table-caption | ruby-base | ruby-text | ruby-base-container | ruby-text-container

<display-box> contents | none

<display-legacy> inline-block | inline-list-item | inline-table | inline-flex | inline-grid

Initial value   inline

Computed value As declared

Applies to   All elements

Description	Defines the kind of display box an element generates during layout. Gratuitous use of display with a document type such as HTML can be tricky, as it upsets the display hierarchy already defined in HTML, but it can also be very useful. In the case of XML, which has no such built-in visual hierarchy, display is indispensable.
	The value none is often used to make elements "disappear," since it removes the element and all of its descendant elements from the presentation. This is true not just in visual media, but in all media; thus, setting an element to display: none will prevent it from being spoken by a speaking browser.
	The value run-in was long a part of CSS2.1 but was dropped in early 2011 because of inconsistencies among browsers. Despite this, it is still listed as part of CSS3.
Examples	h1 {display: block;} li {display: list-item;} img {display: inline;} .hide {display: none;} tr {display: table-row;}

empty-cells
Inh. Y Anim. N

Values	show	hide
Initial value	show
Computed value	As declared
Applies to	Elements with the display value table-cell
Description	Defines the presentation of table cells that contain no content. If shown, the cell's borders and background are drawn. This property is only honored if border-collapse is set to separate; otherwise, it is ignored.
Example	th, td {empty-cells: show;}
Note	empty-cells has no effect unless the value of border-collapse is separate.

filter   Inh. N Anim. Y

Values	[none | blur() | brightness() | contrast() | drop-shadow() | grayscale() | hue-rotate() | invert() | opacity() | sepia() | saturate() | url()]#
Initial value	none
Computed value	As declared
Applies to	All elements (in SVG, applies to all graphics elements and all container elements except the defs element)
Description	Applies a visual filter to the element, resulting in an alteration of its final appearance. url() values point to filter elements in SVG files, either externally or embedded within the HTML document. SVG filters can be quite complex and powerful.

Examples	`img.oldschool {filter: sepia(0.9);}`
	`h2.glowshadow {filter:`
	`    drop-shadow(0 0 0.5em yellow)`
	`    drop-shadow(0.5em 0.75em 30px gray);}`
	`div.logo {filter:`
	`    url(/assets/filters.svg#spotlight);}`

flex   Inh. N Anim. P

Values	[*<flex-grow>* *<flex-shrink>*? ‖ *<flex-basis>*] | none
Initial value	0 1 auto
Computed value	Refer to individual properties
Percentages	Valid for the flex-basis value only, relative to the element's parent's inner main axis size
Applies to	Flex items (children of flex containers)
Animatable	Refer to individual flex properties to see which are animatable
Description	A shorthand property encompassing the flex-grow, flex-shrink, and flex-basis properties, used to set the proportion and types of flexibility permitted

for a flex item. The minimum valid value is a flex basis on its own, in which case the growth and shrink factors are set to their defaults of 0 and 1, respectively. Including the growth and shrink factors is optional, but if one is included, the other *must* also be present.

Examples	`/* sets grow at 1, shrink at 0, basis at auto */`
	`nav ul li {flex: 1 0 auto;}`
	`/* sets grow at 0, shrink at 1, basis at 50% */`
	`ol.gallery li {flex: 50%;}`
	`#invalid {flex: 1 33.%;}  /* INVALID */`

Note	It is *strongly* recommended that authors use this property instead of the separate properties it encompasses.

flex-basis   Inh. N   Anim. P

Values	content | [*<length>* | *<percentage>* | auto]
Initial value	`auto`
Computed value	As declared, with length values made absolute
Percentages	Relative to the flex container's inner main axis size
Applies to	Flex items (children of flex containers)
Animatable	*<length>* and *<percentage>* values only
Description	Defines the initial size of a flex item, used as a basis for all subsequent flex sizing calculations. This can override an explicitly assigned width value for the element.

Examples	`nav ul li {flex-basis: 50%;}`
	`ol.gallery li {flex-basis: 300px;}`
	`div span.whatevs {flex-basis: auto;}`

Note	It is *strongly* recommended that instead of this property, authors use the flex shorthand property to set an item's flex basis.

flex-direction   Inh. N Anim. N

Values	row | row-reverse | column | column-reverse
Initial value	row
Computed value	As declared
Applies to	Flex containers
Description	Defines the direction in which flex items will be flowed into the flex container, which in turn defines how the flex lines will fill the flex container.

Examples	`div.gallery {display: flex; flex-direction: row;}`
	`section.appetizers {display: flex;`
	`    flex-direction: column;}`

flex-flow   Inh. N Anim. N

Values	*<flex-direction>* || *<flex-wrap>*
Initial value	row nowrap
Computed value	As declared
Applies to	Flex containers
Description	A shorthand property encompassing the flex-direction and flex-wrap properties. Note that the default wrapping value is nowrap (see flex-wrap).

Examples	`div.gallery {display: flex; flex-flow: row wrap;}`
	`nav.sidenav {display: flex;`
	`    flex-flow: column nowrap;}`

flex-grow   Inh. N Anim. Y

Values	*<number>*
Initial value	0
Computed value	As declared
Applies to	Flex items (children of flex containers)
Description	Sets the *growth factor* for a flex item. The value supplied is summed up with all the growth factors of

the other flex items in the same flex line, and the
amount they grow is scaled in proportion to their
growth factors as a percentage of the whole.

Examples
```
nav ul li {flex-grow: 1;}
ol.gallery li {flex-grow: 0;}  /* NO growing */
div span.whatevs {flex-grow: 0.5;}
```

Note
It is *strongly* recommended that instead of this property, authors use the flex shorthand property to set
an item's flex growth factor.

flex-shrink   Inh. N   Anim. Y

Values	*<number>*
Initial value	1
Computed value	As declared
Applies to	Flex items (children of flex containers)
Description	Sets the *shrink factor* for a flex item. The value sup-
	plied is summed up with all the shrink factors of the
	other flex items in the same flex line, and the
	amount they shrink is scaled proportional to their
	shrink factors as a percentage of the whole.
Examples	```nav ul li {flex-shrink: 0;} /* NO shrinking */```
	```ol.gallery li {flex-shrink: 0.5;}```
	```div span.whatevs {flex-shrink: 1;}```
Note	It is *strongly* recommended that instead of this prop-
	erty, authors use the flex shorthand property to set
	an item's flex shrink factor.

flex-wrap   Inh. N   Anim. N

Values	nowrap | wrap | wrap-reverse
Initial value	nowrap
Computed value	As declared
Applies to	Flex containers

Description	Defines whether flex items can wrap to multiple flex lines, or only a single flex line is allowed. In a way, it is analogous to white-space wrapping in text content. Note, however, that the default is nowrap, so flex items will keep going in a single line (either a row or a column) even if that means they continue outside the flex container. If you want your flex items to wrap to a new flex line when they run out of room (as in an image gallery), make sure to wrap them.
Examples	`div.gallery {display: flex; flex-wrap: wrap;}` `nav.sidenav {display: flex; flex-wrap: nowrap;}`

float   Inh. N Anim. N

Values	left | right | none
Initial value	none
Computed value	As declared
Applies to	All elements
Description	Defines the direction in which an element is floated. This has traditionally been applied to images in order to let text flow around them, but in CSS, any element may be floated. A floated element will generate a block-level box no matter what kind of element it may be. Floated nonreplaced elements should be given an explicit width, as they otherwise tend to become as narrow as possible. Floating is generally well supported by all browsers, but the nature of floats can lead to unexpected results when they are used as a page layout mechanism. This is largely due to subtle differences in the interpretation of statements like "as narrow as possible."
Examples	`img.figure {float: left;}` `p.sidebar {float: right; width: 15em;}`

font   Inh. Y Anim. P

Values	[[*\<font-style>* ‖ [normal | small-caps] ‖ *\<font-weight>*]? *\<font-size>* [/ *\<line-height>*]? *\<font-family>*] | caption | icon | menu | message-box | small-caption | status-bar
Initial value	Refer to individual properties
Computed value	See individual properties (font-style, etc.)
Percentages	Calculated with respect to the parent element for *\<font-size>* and with respect to the element's *\<font-size>* for *\<line-height>*
Applies to	All elements
Animatable	Refer to individual font properties to see which are animatable
Description	A shorthand property used to set all the aspects of an element's font at once. It can also be used to set the element's font to match an aspect of the user's computing environment using keywords such as icon. If keywords are not used, the minimum font value *must* include the font size and family *in that order*, and any font value that is not a keyword must end with the font family. Otherwise, the font declaration will be ignored.

Examples	`p {font: small-caps italic bold small/`
	`  1.25em Helvetica,sans-serif;}`
	`p.example {font: 14px Arial;} /* technically`
	`  correct, although generic font-families`
	`  are encouraged for fallback purposes */`
	`.figure span {font: icon;}`

font-family   Inh. Y Anim. N

Values	[*\<family-name>* | *\<generic-family>*]#
Initial value	User agent–specific
Computed value	As declared
Applies to	All elements

Description	Defines a font family to be used in the display of an element's text. Note that use of a specific font family (e.g., Geneva) is wholly dependent on that family being available, either on the user's computer or thanks to a downloadable font file, and the font family containing the glyphs needed to display the content. Therefore, using generic family names as a fallback is strongly encouraged. Font names that contain spaces or nonalphabetic characters should be quoted to minimize potential confusion. In contrast, generic fallback family names should *never* be quoted.
| **Examples** | ```
p {font-family: Helvetica, Arial, sans-serif;}
li {font-family: Georgia, Times, TimesNR,
    "New Century Schoolbook", serif;}
pre {font-family: Consolas, "Courier New",
    "Andale Mono", Monaco, monospace;}
``` |

font-feature-settings   Inh. Y Anim. N

Values	normal | <*feature-tag-value*>#
Initial value	normal
Computed value	As declared
Applies to	All elements
Description	Used to turn font features on and off; examples include ligatures, old-style numbers, and more. Whether a font feature actually can be enabled depends entirely on the font face being used: turning ligatures on or off can only work if the face has defined ligatures in the first place.
| **Examples** | ```
h1 {font-feature-settings: "liga";}
ol {font-feature-settings: "liga" on, "smcp" on,
    "zero" on;}
``` |
| **Note** | Has a corresponding @font-face descriptor. |

font-kerning

Values	auto | normal | none
Initial value	auto
Computed value	As declared
Applies to	All elements
Description	In effect, allows the author to disable kerning of text for a given element. The default of auto tells user agents to do what they normally do, whatever that is. normal directs the user agent to use any kerning information in the font face to kern text, even if it normally wouldn't. With none, kerning is disabled, even if the face has kerning information and the user agent would make use of it. Note that kerning is done *before* any letter spacing is altered (see letter-spacing).
Examples	body {kerning: normal;} div.typewriter {kerning: none;}
Note	Has a corresponding @font-face descriptor.

font-size

Values	xx-small | x-small | small | medium | large | x-large | xx-large | smaller | larger | *<length>* | *<percentage>*
Initial value	medium
Computed value	For length values, the absolute length; otherwise, as declared
Percentages	Calculated with respect to the parent element's font size
Applies to	All elements
Animatable	*<length>* and *<percentage>* values only
Description	Defines the size of the font. The size can be defined as an absolute size, a relative size, a length value, or a

percentage value. Negative length and percentage values are not permitted. The dangers of font size assignment are many and varied, and use of points is particularly discouraged in web design as there is no certain relationship between points and the pixels on a screen. It's a matter of historical interest that because of early misunderstandings, setting the font-size to medium led to different results in early versions of Internet Explorer and Navigator 4.x.

Examples
```
h2 {font-size: 200%;}
code {font-size: 0.9em;}
p.caption {font-size: 9px;}
```

font-size-adjust   Inh. Y   Anim. Y

Values	*<number>* | none
Initial value	none
Computed value	As declared
Applies to	All elements
Description	Defines an *aspect value* for the element, which is used to scale fonts such that they more closely match each other in cases where fallback fonts are used. The proper aspect value for a font is its true x-height divided by its font size.
Examples	body {font-family: Helvetica, sans-serif; font-size-adjust: 0.53;}

font-stretch   Inh. Y   Anim. N

Values	normal | ultra-condensed | extra-condensed | condensed | semi-condensed | semi-expanded | expanded | extra-expanded | ultra-expanded
Initial value	normal
Computed value	As declared
Applies to	All elements

Description	Replaces a given font face with a narrower or wider variant, but *only* if the face has narrower or wider variants defined. User agents will not programmatically stretch or squeeze a face, but only swap in a variant face (if it exists).
Examples	`h1.bigtext {font-stretch: ultra-expanded;}` `caption.meme {font-stretch: condensed;}`
Note	Has a corresponding @font-face descriptor.

font-style   Inh. Y Anim. N

Values	italic	oblique	normal
Initial value	normal
Computed value	As declared
Applies to	All elements
Description	Defines whether the font uses an italic, oblique, or normal font face. Italic text is generally defined as a separate face within the font family. It is theoretically possible for a user agent to compute a slanted font face from the normal face. In reality, user agents rarely (if at all) recognize the difference between italic and oblique text and almost always render both in exactly the same way.
Examples	`em {font-style: oblique;}` `i {font-style: italic;}`
Note	Has a corresponding @font-face descriptor.

font-synthesis   Inh. Y Anim. N

Values	none	[weight ‖ style]
Initial value	weight style
Computed value	As declared
Applies to	All elements
Description	Defines whether user agents are permitted to programmatically generate bold or italic variants for

fonts that don't have bold or italic faces. This is generally frowned upon by typographers, and the results can be visually displeasing, but it does permit visual emphasis of text in font families that lack the necessary faces. If you don't want to risk it, use none to suppress this behavior.

Examples
```
h1 {font-synthesis: none;}
pre code {font-synthesis: style;}
```

font-variant   Inh. Y Anim. N

Values (CSS2.1)   normal | small-caps

Values (Level 3)   normal | none | [<common-lig-values> ‖ <discretionary-lig-values> ‖ <historical-lig-values> ‖ <contextual-alt-values> ‖ stylistic(<feature-value-name>) ‖ historical-forms ‖ styleset(<feature-value-name>#) ‖ character-variant(<feature-value-name>#) ‖ swash(<feature-value-name>) ‖ ornaments(<feature-value-name>) ‖ annotation(<feature-value-name>) ‖ [small-caps | all-small-caps | petite-caps | all-petite-caps | unicase | titling-caps] ‖ <numeric-figure-values> ‖ <numeric-spacing-values> ‖ <numeric-fraction-values> ‖ ordinal ‖ slashed-zero ‖ <east-asian-variant-values> ‖ <east-asian-width-values> ‖ ruby]

Initial value   normal

Computed value   As declared

Applies to   All elements

Description   Defines whether text is set in the small-caps style. It is theoretically possible for a user agent to compute a small-caps font face from the normal face.

Examples
```
h3 {font-variant: small-caps;}
p {font-variant: normal;}
```

Note   Has a corresponding @font-face descriptor.

font-weight
                                                          Inh. Y Anim. N

Values	normal | bold | bolder | lighter | 100 | 200 | 300 | 400 | 500 | 600 | 700 | 800 | 900
Initial value	normal
Computed value	One of the numeric values (100, etc.), or one of the numeric values plus one of the relative values (bolder or lighter)
Applies to	All elements
Description	Defines the font weight used in rendering an element's text. The numeric value 400 is equivalent to the keyword normal, and 700 is equivalent to bold. If a font has only two weights—normal and bold— the numbers 100 through 500 will be normal, and 600 through 900 will be bold. In general terms, the visual result of each numeric value must be at least as light as the next lowest number and at least as heavy as the next highest number.
Examples	b {font-weight: 700;} strong {font-weight: bold;} .delicate {font-weight: lighter;}
Note	Has a corresponding @font-face descriptor.

grid
                                                          Inh. N Anim. N

Values	none | subgrid | [*<grid-template-rows>* / *<grid-template-columns>*] | [*<line-names>*? *<string>* *<track-size>*? *<line-names>*?]+ [/ *<track-list>*]?] | [*<grid-auto-flow>* [*<grid-auto-rows>* [/ *<grid-auto-columns>*]?]?]]
Initial value	See individual properties
Computed value	See individual properties
Applies to	Grid containers
Description	A shorthand property allowing the almost complete definition of an element's grid system, not counting

grid gaps. The value syntax can become quite complex and, for clarity's sake, most authors rely on the individual properties instead of grid, but there are no technical reasons to avoid grid.

Example

```
body {display: grid;
    grid:
        "header header header header" 3em
        ". content sidebar ." 1fr
        "footer footer footer footer" 5em /
        2em 3fr minmax(10em,1fr) 2em;}
```

grid-area   Inh. N   Anim. N

Values   *<grid-line>* [/ *<grid-line>*]{0,3}

Initial value   See individual properties

Computed value As declared

Applies to   Grid items and absolutely positioned elements, if their containing block is a grid container

Description   Used to assign a grid item to a specific area of a defined grid. This can be done using a single identifier, or using slash-separated grid line identifiers. If all four grid lines are supplied, they are given in the order row-start (top) / column-start (left) / row-end (bottom) / column-end (right), which is the reverse of the usual top-right-bottom-left order for margins, padding, and so on.

Examples   ```
#masthead {grid-area: header;}
#sidebar {grid-area: 1 / 2 / 1 / 3;}
```

## grid-auto-columns                             Inh. N   Anim. N

**Values**          *<track-breadth>* | minmax(*<track-breadth>*, *<track-breadth>*)

**Definition**

*<track-breadth>*   *<length>* | *<percentage>* | *<flex>* | min-content | max-content | auto

**Initial value**   auto
```

Computed value	Depends on the specific track sizing
Applies to	Grid containers
Description	Defines the sizing of column tracks for columns that are automatically generated; that is, columns that are created because a grid item needs to be placed outside the explicitly defined grid columns.

Example	`div.grid {display: grid;`
	`    grid-template-rows: 80px 80px;`
	`    grid-template-columns: 20em 1fr;`
	`    grid-auto-columns: 20em;}`

grid-auto-flow   Inh. N Anim. N

Values	[row | column] ‖ dense
Initial value	row
Computed value	As declared
Applies to	Grid containers
Description	Defines the direction in which grid items that have not been explicitly assigned to a grid area using `grid-area` or the `grid-column` and `grid-row` properties will be automatically flowed into the grid container.
Examples	`section.menu {grid-auto-flow: column;}` `div.gallery {grid-auto-flow: row dense;}`

grid-auto-rows   Inh. N Anim. N

Values	*<track-breadth>* | minmax(*<track-breadth>*, *<track-breadth>*)
Definition	
<track-breadth>	*<length>* | *<percentage>* | *<flex>* | min-content | max-content | auto
Initial value	auto
Computed value	Depends on the specific track sizing
Applies to	Grid containers

Description	Defines the sizing of row tracks for rows that are automatically generated; that is, rows that are created because a grid item needs to be placed outside the explicitly defined grid rows.
| Example | ```
div.grid {display: grid;
    grid-template-rows: 80px 80px;
    grid-template-columns: 20em 1fr;
    grid-auto-rows: 80px;}
``` |

grid-column   Inh. N Anim. N

Values	*<grid-line>* [/ *<grid-line>*]?
Definition	
<grid-line>	auto | *<identifier>* | [*<integer>* && *<identifier>*?] | [span && [*<integer>* || *<identifier>*]]
Initial value	auto
Computed value	As declared
Applies to	Grid items and absolutely positioned elements, if their containing block is a grid container
Description	Acts as a shorthand property encompassing the grid-column-start and grid-column-end properties. When a single number or identifier is given, the second is assumed to be the span 1 (for a number) or the same identifier. Negative numeric grid lines count backward from the end of the explicit grid (generally the right side).
| Examples | ```
header {grid-column: 1 / -1;}
#sidebar {grid-column: 1 / span 2;}
footer {grid-column: footer / 4;}
``` |

grid-column-end   Inh. N Anim. N

Values	auto | *<custom-ident>* | [*<integer>* && *<custom-ident>*?] | [span && [*<integer>* || *<custom-ident>*]]
Initial value	auto

Computed value	As declared
Applies to	Grid items and absolutely positioned elements, if their containing block is a grid container
Description	Defines the column grid line on which an element's layout ends, or (when using the span keyword) the number of column tracks, or identified column tracks, the element spans.

Examples	`header {grid-column-end: main-content;}`
	`#sidebar {grid-column-end: span 2;}`
	`footer {grid-column-end: 4;}`

grid-column-gap   Inh. N Anim. Y

Values	*<length>*	*<percentage>*
Initial value	0
Computed value	An absolute length
Applies to	Grid containers
Description	Sets a gap distance between column tracks. This permits an author to force open gaps between column tracks, even when the grid items have no margins to push them away from each other. The gap size is the same for all column gaps.
Example	`#grid {display: grid; grid-column-gap: 1em;}`
Note	As of early 2018, the CSS Working Group intends to change this property to simply `column-gap` and have it apply to multicolumn and flex containers as well as grid containers.

grid-column-start   Inh. N Anim. N

Values	auto	*<custom-ident>*	[*<integer>* && *<custom-ident>*?]	[span && [*<integer>* ‖ *<custom-ident>*]]
Initial value	auto
Computed value	As declared

Applies to	Grid items and absolutely positioned elements, if their containing block is a grid container
Description	Defines the column grid line on which an element's layout starts, by means of either a grid line number or an identifier. If the span keyword is used, the grid item spans back from the grid line defined by grid-column-end.

Examples	`header {grid-column-start: masthead;}`
	`#sidebar {grid-column-start: span 1;}`
	`footer {grid-column-start: -2;}`

grid-gap   Inh. N   Anim. Y

Values	*<grid-row-gap>* *<grid-column-gap>*
Initial value	0 0
Computed value	As declared
Applies to	Grid containers
Description	A shorthand property encompassing the grid-row-gap and grid-column-gap properties, in that order. If only one value is supplied, the value is assumed to be the same for both row and column gaps.
Examples	`#grid {display: grid; grid-gap: 12px 1em;}` `div.gallery {display: grid; grid-gap: 2.5vw;}`
Note	As of early 2018, the CSS Working Group intends to change this property to simply gap and have it apply to multicolumn and flex containers as well as grid containers.

grid-row   Inh. N   Anim. N

Values	*<grid-line>* [/ *<grid-line>*]?
Definition	
<grid-line>	auto | *<identifier>* | [*<integer>* && *<identifier>*?] | [span && [*<integer>* || *<identifier>*]]
Initial value	auto

Computed value	As declared
Applies to	Grid items and absolutely positioned elements, if their containing block is a grid container
Description	Acts as a shorthand property encompassing the `grid-row-start` and `grid-row-end` properties. When a single number or identifier is declared, the second is assumed to be the `span 1` (for a number) or the same identifier.

Examples	`#sidebar {grid-row: 1 / -1;}`
	`footer {grid-row: footer-start / footer-end;}`
	`header {grid-row: top;}`
	`   /* a trailing '/ span 1' is assumed */`

grid-row-end   Inh. N Anim. N

Values	auto | *<custom-ident>* | [*<integer>* && *<custom-ident>*?] | [span && [*<integer>* ‖ *<custom-ident>*]]
Initial value	auto
Computed value	As declared
Applies to	Grid items and absolutely positioned elements, if their containing block is a grid container
Description	Defines the row grid line on which an element's layout ends, or (when using the `span` keyword) the number of row tracks, or identified row tracks, the element spans across.

Examples	`header {grid-row-end: span 1;}`
	`#sidebar {grid-row-end: -1;}`
	`footer {grid-row-end: footer-end;}`

grid-row-gap   Inh. N Anim. Y

Values	*<length>* | *<percentage>*
Initial value	0
Computed value	An absolute length
Applies to	Grid containers

Description	Sets a gap distance between row tracks. This permits an author to force open gaps between row tracks, even when the grid items have no margins to push them away from each other. The gap size is the same for all row gaps.
Example	`#grid {display: grid; grid-row-gap: 12px;}`
Note	As of early 2018, the CSS Working Group intends to change this property to simply `row-gap` and have it apply to multicolumn and flex containers as well as grid containers.

grid-row-start   Inh. N Anim. N

Values	auto | *<custom-ident>* | [*<integer>* && *<custom-ident>*?] | [span && [*<integer>* || *<custom-ident>*]]
Initial value	auto
Computed value	As declared
Applies to	Grid items and absolutely positioned elements, if their containing block is a grid container
Description	Defines the row grid line on which an element's layout starts, by means of either a grid line number or an identifier. If the span keyword is used, this means the grid item spans back from the grid line defined by grid-row-end.

Examples	`header {grid-row-start: masthead;}`
	`#sidebar {grid-row-start: span 1;}`
	`footer {grid-row-start: footer-start;}`

grid-template-areas   Inh. N Anim. N

Values	none | *<string>*
Initial value	none
Computed value	As declared
Applies to	Grid containers

Description	This property allows the author to create an explicit grid system using strings of text to define the names and placement of grid areas. This allows for a much more visual representation of the grid areas in a grid container, and automatically creating named grid lines to make the grid areas work. Because the areas are defined using patterns of text, no areas defined with this property can overlap.

Examples	`#grid {display: grid;`
	`    grid-template-areas:`
	`        "h h h h"`
	`        "l c c r"`
	`        "l f f f";}`
	`#grid2 {display: grid;`
	`    grid-template-areas:`
	`        "header  header header  header"`
	`        "leftside content content rightside"`
	`        "leftside footer  footer  footer";}`

grid-template-columns   Inh. N   Anim. N

Values	none | *<track-list>* | *<auto-track-list>*
Initial value	none
Computed value	As declared, with lengths made absolute
Percentages	Refer to the inline size (usually width) of the grid container
Applies to	Grid containers
Description	Provides authors a way to define grid line names and track sizes for columns in the explicit grid.

Examples	`aside {grid-template-columns:`
	`    max-content min-content max-content;}`
	`article {grid-template-columns:`
	`    15em 4.5fr 3fr 10%;}`
	`section {grid-template-columns:`
	`    [start col-a] 200px [col-b] 50% [col-c] 1fr`
	`    [stop end last];}`

grid-template-rows   Inh. N Anim. N

Values	none | *<track-list>* | *<auto-track-list>*
Initial value	none
Computed value	As declared, with lengths made absolute
Percentages	Refer to the block size (usually height) of the grid container
Applies to	Grid containers
Description	Provides authors a way to define grid line names and track sizes for rows in the explicit grid.

Examples	`aside {grid-template-rows: 200px 50% 100px;}`
	`article {grid-template-rows:`
	`   3em minmax(5em,1fr) 2em;}`
	`section {grid-template-rows:`
	`   [start masthead] 3em [content] calc(100%-5em)`
	`   [footer] 2em [stop end];}`

height   Inh. N Anim. Y

Values	*<length>* | *<percentage>* | auto
Initial value	auto
Computed value	For auto and percentage values, as declared; otherwise, an absolute length, unless the property does not apply to the element (then auto)
Percentages	Calculated with respect to the height of the containing block (when valid)
Applies to	All elements except nonreplaced inline elements, table rows, and row groups
Description	Defines the total height of portions of an element; the exact portions depend on the value of box-sizing. Negative length and percentage values are not permitted.
Examples	`img.icon {height: 50px;}` `h1 {height: 1.75em;}`

hyphens

Values	manual | auto | none
Initial value	manual
Computed value	As declared
Animatabale	No
Applies to	All elements
Description	Used to declare whether the hyphenation of words at line breaks must be done manually (e.g., with a "soft hyphen"—­ or U+00AD—inserted into the document) or can be done automatically by the user agent. In the case of none, all hyphenation is suppressed, even when hinted manually in the document. Automatic hyphenation is heavily language-dependent, and may vary greatly between user agents.
Examples	h1, h2 {hyphens: none;} aside.poem {hyphens: manual;}

isolation

Values	auto | isolate
Initial value	auto
Computed value	As declared
Applies to	All elements (in SVG, it applies to container elements, graphics elements, and graphics-referencing elements)
Description	Determines whether an element creates an isolated blending context. An isolated element will only blend with itself; that is, the foreground portions of the element will blend with the background portions of that same element, but *not* with the backdrop of its parent element or any other elements that might appear behind it. The visual effect can be similar to that of a document loaded into an iframe element,

though this analogy is not exact: the isolated element still inherits styles from its ancestors.

Example   p.alone {isolation: isolate;}

---

justify-content   Inh. N Anim. N

Values	flex-start | flex-end | center | space-between | space-around | space-evenly
Initial value	flex-start
Conputed value	As declared
Applies to	Flex containers
Description	Defines the distribution of flex items along the main axis of a flex container.
Examples	nav {justify-content: space-evenly;} div.gallery {justify-content: space-between;}
Note	As of early 2018, there are plans to have this property apply to many (or all) elements, not just flex containers, and be given the values start and end to replicate flex-start and flex-end behavior for non-flex environments.

---

left   Inh. N Anim. P

Values	<length> | <percentage> | auto
Initial value	auto
Computed value	For static elements, auto; for length values, the corresponding absolute length; for percentage values, the specified value; otherwise, auto
Percentages	Refer to the height of the containing block for top and bottom, and the width of the containing block for right and left
Applies to	Positioned elements
Animatable	<length> and <percentage> values only

| Description | Defines the offset between the left outer margin edge of an absolutely positioned element and the left edge of its containing block; or, for relatively positioned elements, the distance by which the element is offset to the right of its starting position. |

| Examples | `div#footer {position: fixed; left: 0;}`
`*.hanger {position: relative; left: -25px;}` |

letter-spacing

Inh. Y Anim. Y

Values	*<length>*	normal
Initial value	normal
Computed value	For length values, the absolute length; otherwise, normal
Applies to	All elements
Description	Defines the amount of whitespace to be inserted between the character boxes of text. Because character glyphs are typically narrower than their character boxes, length values create a modifier to the usual spacing between letters. Thus, normal is (most likely) synonymous with 0. Negative length and percentage values are permitted and will cause letters to bunch closer together.

Examples	`p.spacious {letter-spacing: 6px;}`
	`em {letter-spacing: 0.2em;}`
	`p.cramped {letter-spacing: -0.5em;}`

line-break

Inh. Y Anim. Y

Values	auto	loose	normal	strict
Initial value	auto
Computed value	As declared
Applies to	All elements
Description	Affects the wrapping of lines of text in CJK (Chinese-Japanese-Korean) text. The precise meanings of loose, normal, and strict are left unde-

fined, so the only solid expectation is that `loose` will use the "least restrictive" line-breaking, `normal` will use the "most common" line-breaking, and `strict` will use the "most stringent" line-breaking.

Example   `div.cjk {line-break: strict;}`

---

line-height   Inh. Y Anim. Y

Values   *<number>* | *<length>* | *<percentage>* | `normal`

Initial value   `normal`

Computed value For length and percentage values, the absolute value; otherwise, as declared

Percentages   Relative to the font size of the element

Applies to   All elements (but see text regarding replaced and block-level elements)

Description   This property influences the layout of line boxes. When applied to a block-level element, it defines the minimum (but not the maximum) distance between baselines within that element. When applied to an inline element, it is used to define the *leading* of that element.

The difference between the computed values of `line-height` and `font-size` (called "leading" in CSS) is split in half and added to the top and bottom of each piece of content in a line of text. The shortest box that can enclose all those pieces of content is the line box.

A raw number value assigns a scaling factor, which is inherited instead of a computed value. Negative values are not permitted.

Examples
```
p {line-height: 1.5em;}
h2 {line-height: 200%;}
ul {line-height: 1.2;}
pre {line-height: 0.75em;}
```

list-style

Inh. Y   Anim. N

Values	[*<list-style-type>* ‖ *<list-style-image>* ‖ *<list-style-position>*]
Initial value	Refer to individual properties
Computed value	See individual properties
Applies to	Elements whose display value is list-item
Description	A shorthand property that defines the marker type, whether a symbol or an image, and its (crude) placement. Because it applies to any element that has a display value of list-item, it will apply only to li elements in ordinary HTML, although it can be applied to any element and subsequently inherited by list-item elements.
| **Examples** | ```
ul {list-style: square url(bullet3.gif) outer;}
    /* values are inherited by 'li' elements */
ol {list-style: upper-roman;}
``` |

list-style-image

Inh. Y   Anim. N

Values	*<uri>* | *<image>* | none
Initial value	none
Computed value	For *<uri>* values, the absolute URI; otherwise, none
Applies to	Elements whose display value is list-item
Description	Specifies an image to be used as the marker on an ordered or unordered list item. The placement of the image with respect to the content of the list item can be crudely controlled using list-style-position.
| **Examples** | ```
ul {list-style-image: url(bullet3.gif);}
ul li {list-style-image:
    url(\http://example.org/pix/checkmark.png);}
``` |

list-style-position

Values	inside | outside
Initial value	outside
Computed value	As declared
Applies to	Elements whose display value is list-item
Description	Defines the position of the list marker with respect to the content of the list item. Outside markers are placed some distance from the border edge of the list item, but the distance is not defined in CSS. Inside markers are treated as though they were inline elements inserted at the beginning of the list item's content.
Examples	li {list-style-position: outside;} ol li {list-style-position: inside;}

list-style-type

Values	disc | circle | square | disclosure-open | disclosure-closed | decimal | decimal-leading-zero | arabic-indic | armenian | upper-armenian | lower-armenian | bengali | cambodian | khmer | cjk-decimal | devanagari | gujarati | gurmukhi | georgian | hebrew | kannada | lao | malayalam | mongolian | myanmar | oriya | persian | lower-roman | upper-roman | tamil | telugu | thai | tibetan | lower-alpha | lower-latin | upper-alpha | upper-latin | cjk-earthly-branch | cjk-heavenly-stem | lower-greek | hiragana | hiragana-iroha | katakana | katakana-iroha | japanese-informal | japanese-formal | korean-hangul-formal | korean-hanja-informal | korean-hanja-formal | simp-chinese-informal | simp-chinese-formal | trad-chinese-informal | trad-chinese-formal | ethiopic-numeric | *<string>* | none

Initial value	disc
Computed value	As declared
Applies to	Elements whose display value is list-item
Description	Defines the type of marker system to be used in the presentation of a list. CSS3 provides a greatly expanded number of list types, but as of early 2018, support for these newer list types has some spotty parts. Use caution when using list types beyond those provided by CSS2.1.
	There is no defined behavior for what happens when a list using an alphabetic ordering exceeds the letters in the list. For example, once an upper-latin list reaches "Z," the specification does not say what the next bullet should be. (Two possible answers are "AA" and "ZA.") This is the case regardless of the alphabet in use. Thus, there is no guarantee that different user agents will act consistently.
Examples	ul {list-style-type: square;} ol {list-style-type: lower-roman;}

margin   Inh. N Anim. Y

Values	[<length> | <percentage> | auto]{1,4}
Initial value	Not defined
Computed value	See individual properties
Percentages	Refer to the width of the containing block
Applies to	All elements
Description	A shorthand property that defines the width of the overall margin for an element or sets distinct widths for the individual side margins. Vertically adjacent margins of block-level elements are collapsed, whereas inline elements effectively do not take top and bottom margins. The left and right margins of inline elements do not collapse, nor do margins on floated elements. Negative margin values are permitted, but caution is warranted because negative values

can cause elements to overlap other elements or to appear to be wider than their parent elements.

Examples
```
h1 {margin: 2ex;}
p {margin: auto;}
img {margin: 10px;}
```

margin-bottom

Inh. N Anim. Y

Values	*<length>* | *<percentage>* | auto
Initial value	0
Computed value	For length values, the absolute length; otherwise, as declared
Percentages	Refer to the width of the containing block
Applies to	All elements
Description	Defines the width of the bottom margin for an element. Negative values are permitted, but caution is warranted (see margin).
Examples	`ul {margin-bottom: 0.5in;}` `h1 {margin-bottom: 2%;}`

margin-left

Inh. N Anim. Y

Values	*<length>* | *<percentage>* | auto
Initial value	0
Computed value	For length values, the absolute length; otherwise, as declared
Percentages	Refer to the width of the containing block
Applies to	All elements
Description	Defines the width of the left margin for an element. Negative values are permitted, but caution is warranted (see margin).
Examples	`p {margin-left: 5%;}` `pre {margin-left: 3em;}`

margin-right   Inh. N   Anim. Y

Values	*\<length\>* | *\<percentage\>* | auto
Initial value	0
Computed value	For length values, the absolute length; otherwise, as declared
Percentages	Refer to the width of the containing block
Applies to	All elements
Description	Defines the width of the right margin for an element. Negative values are permitted, but caution is warranted (see margin).
Examples	`img {margin-right: 30px;}` `ol {margin-right: 5em;}`

margin-top   Inh. N   Anim. Y

Values	*\<length\>* | *\<percentage\>* | auto
Initial value	0
Computed value	For length values, the absolute length; otherwise, as declared
Percentages	Refer to the width of the containing block
Applies to	All elements
Description	Defines the width of the top margin for an element. Negative values are permitted, but caution is warranted (see margin).
Examples	`ul {margin-top: 0.5in;}` `h3 {margin-top: 1.5em;}`

mask   Inh. N   Anim. P

Values	[*\<mask-image\>* ‖ *\<mask-position\>* [/ *\<mask-size\>*]? ‖ *\<mask-repeat\>* ‖ *\<mask-clip\>* ‖ *\<mask-origin\>* ‖ *\<mask-composite\>* ‖ *\<mask-mode\>*]#
Initial value	See individual properties

Computed value	As declared
Applies to	All elements (in SVG, applies to all graphics elements and all container elements except the defs element)
Animatable	Refer to individual mask properties to see which are animatable
Description	A shorthand property encompassing all the other image masking properties. It is analogous to background as compared to the various background properties, and many of the masking and background properties share values and behaviors.
Examples	```img.masked {mask:
url(#mask) no-repeat center/cover luminance;}
#example {mask:
url(c.svg) repeat-y top left / auto subtract,
url(s.png) no-repeat center / 50% 33% add,
url(t.gif) repeat-y 25% 67% / contain add;
}```

mask-clip   Inh. N Anim. N

Values	[content-box | padding-box | border-box | margin-box | fill-box | stroke-box | view-box | no-clip]#
Initial value	border-box
Computed value	As declared
Applies to	All elements (in SVG, applies to all graphics elements and all container elements except the defs element)
Description	Defines the outer edge of the visible portions of an element's mask, as an aspect of the element's box model. This allows authors to apply a masking shape to an element but then further reduce the visible parts of the element without having to directly alter the mask shape.
Examples	```p:nth-child(1) {mask-clip: border-box;}
p:nth-child(2) {mask-clip: padding-box;}
p:nth-child(3) {mask-clip: content-box;}```

---

mask-composite   Inh. N   Anim. N

Values   [add | subtract | intersect | exclude]#

Initial value   add

Computed value As declared

Applies to   All elements (in SVG, applies to all graphics ele-
                    ments and all container elements except the defs
                    element)

Description   Controls the way multiple masks are combined, with
                    the result sometimes dependent on the order of the
                    mask shapes. For example, if a square mask is atop a
                    circular mask and the value of mask-composite is
                    subtract, then the circle is subtracted from the
                    square. If the order is reversed so the circle is atop
                    the square, then the square is subtracted from the
                    circle. For the other values, the result should not
                    depend on the masks' stacking order.

Examples   img.masked {mask-composite: add;}
                    span.mask3 {mask-composite: subtract, add, add;}

mask-image   Inh. N   Anim. N

Values   [none | <image> | <mask-source>]#

Definitions

<image>   Any of the value types <uri>, <image()>, <image-
                    set()>, <element()>, <cross-fade()>, or <gradient>

<mask-source>   A url() that points to a mask element in an SVG
                    image

Initial value   none

Computed value As declared

Applies to   All elements (in SVG, applies to all graphics ele-
                    ments and all container elements except the defs
                    element)

Description   Applies an image, or a portion of an SVG image, to
                    an element as a masking shape. The result is that the

masked element has portions of itself made invisible, while others are wholly or partially visible. The exact visual result will depend on the value of mask-mode; by default, the alpha channel of the mask-image will be used to determine the masking of the element.

Examples	`*.masked.compass {mask-image: url(Compass.png);}`
	`*.masked.theatre {mask-image:`
	`    url(theatre-masks.svg);}`

mask-mode   Inh. N   Anim. N

Values	[alpha | luminance | match-source]#
Initial value	match-source
Computed value	As declared
Applies to	All elements (in SVG, applies to all graphics elements and all container elements except the defs element)
Description	Determines which aspect of a masking image is used to determine its masking shape: its transparency or its brightness. If alpha is used, then any part of the masking image with no transparency reveal the masked element, whereas any part of the mask with full transparency hides the masked element. Transparency values between the two show the masked element, but set to the masking image's opacity level. For luminance, the brightness of the masking image is treated as transparency is for alpha: full brightness fully reveals the masked element, full darkness hides it, and in-between brightness reveal the masked element with some transparency. match-source means the same as alpha *unless* the masking source is an SVG mask element, in which case it's the same as luminance.
Examples	`p {mask-mode: alpha;}` `img.lum {mask-mode: luminance, alpha;}`

mask-origin

Inh. N Anim. N

Values	[content-box | padding-box | border-box | margin-box | fill-box | stroke-box | view-box]#
Initial value	border-box
Computed value	As declared
Applies to	All elements (in SVG, applies to all graphics elements and all container elements except the defs element)
Description	Changes the origin box for the masking image as applied to the masked element. This allows the author to vary the initial placement of the mask before sizing, repeating, or positioning it.
Examples	div.inset {mask-origin: content-box;} svg#radio {mask-origin: stroke-box, fill-box;}

mask-position

Inh. N Anim. P

Values	*<position>*#
Initial value	0% 0%
Computed value	As declared
Applies to	All elements (in SVG, applies to all graphics elements and all container elements except the defs element)
Animatable	*<length>* and *<percentage>* values only
Description	Allows authors to position a masking image in a manner identical to the positioning of background images. The default will place the masking image in the top-left corner of the box defined by mask-origin.
Examples	p:nth-child(1) {mask-position: top right;} p:nth-child(2) {mask-position: 33% 80%;} p:nth-child(3) {mask-position: 5em 120%;}

mask-repeat   Inh. N   Anim. Y

Values	[repeat-x | repeat-y | [repeat | space | round | no-repeat]{1,2}]#
Initial value	repeat
Computed value	As declared
Applies to	All elements (in SVG, applies to all graphics elements and all container elements except the defs element)
Description	Allows authors to repeat a masking image in a manner identical to the repetition of background images. Note that the default is to repeat a mask in all directions.
Examples	p:nth-child(1) {mask-repeat: repeat;} p:nth-child(2) {mask-repeat: repeat round;} p:nth-child(3) {mask-repeat: space no-repeat;}

mask-size   Inh. N   Anim. P

Values	[[<length> | <percentage> | auto]{1,2} | cover | contain]#
Initial value	auto
Computed value	As declared, with length values converted to absolute lengths
Applies to	All elements (in SVG, applies to all graphics elements and all container elements except the defs element)
Animatable	<length> and <percentage> values only
Description	Sets the size of the initial masking image in a manner identical to the sizing of background images.
Examples	p:nth-child(1) {mask-size: 80%;} p:nth-child(2) {mask-size: 2em 3em, 100%;} p:nth-child(3) {mask-size: cover, 100%, contain;}

mask-type   Inh. N   Anim. N

Values	luminance | alpha
Initial value	luminance
Computed value	As declared
Applies to	SVG mask elements
Description	Sets the blending mode when the masking image is defined by an SVG mask element as opposed to, say, a PNG file or an entire SVG. Of interest because most masking images use the alpha blending mode, but mask element masks default to luminance.
Example	svg #mask {mask-type: alpha;}

max-height   Inh. N   Anim. P

Values	<length> | <percentage> | none
Initial value	none
Computed value	For percentages, as declared; for length values, the absolute length; otherwise, none
Percentages	Refer to the height of the containing block
Applies to	All elements except nonreplaced inline elements and table elements
Animatable	<length> and <percentage> values only
Description	Defines a maximum constraint on the height of the element (the exact nature of that height is dependent on the value of box-sizing). Thus, the element can be shorter than the declared value but not taller. Negative values are not permitted.
Example	div#footer {max-height: 3em;}

max-width   Inh. N   Anim. P

Values	<length> | <percentage> | none
Initial value	none

Computed value	For percentages, as declared; for length values, the absolute length; otherwise, none
Percentages	Refer to the height of the containing block
Applies to	All elements except nonreplaced inline elements and table elements
Animatable	*<length>* and *<percentage>* values only
Description	Defines a maximum constraint on the width of the element (the exact nature of that width is dependent on the value of box-sizing). Thus, the element can be narrower than the declared value but not wider. Negative values are not permitted.
Example	`#sidebar img {width: 50px; max-width: 100%;}`

min-height   Inh. N   Anim. Y

Values	*<length>*	*<percentage>*
Initial value	0
Computed value	For percentages, as declared; for length values, the absolute length
Percentages	Refer to the width of the containing block
Applies to	All elements except nonreplaced inline elements and table elements
Description	Defines a minimum constraint on the height of the element (the exact nature of that height is dependent on the value of box-sizing). Thus, the element can be taller than the declared value, but not shorter. Negative values are not permitted.
Example	`div#footer {min-height: 1em;}`

min-width   Inh. N   Anim. Y

Values	*<length>*	*<percentage>*
Initial value	0

Computed value	For percentages, as declared; for length values, the absolute length
Percentages	Refer to the width of the containing block
Applies to	All elements except nonreplaced inline elements and table elements
Description	Defines a minimum constraint on the width of the element (the exact nature of that width is dependent on the value of box-sizing). Thus, the element can be wider than the declared value, but not narrower. Negative values are not permitted.
Example	`div.aside {width: 13em; max-width: 33%;}`

mix-blend-mode   Inh. N Anim. N

Values	normal | multiply | screen | overlay | darken | lighten | color-dodge | color-burn | hard-light | soft-light | difference | exclusion | hue | saturation | color | luminosity
Initial value	normal
Computed value	As declared
Applies to	All elements
Description	Changes how an element is composited with its backdrop. The "backdrop" consists of any ancestor backgrounds and other elements that are "behind" the element being styled. The default of normal imposes simple alpha blending, as CSS has permitted since its inception. The others cause the element and its backdrop to be combined in various ways; for example, lighten means that the final result will show, at each pixel, either the element or its backdrop, whichever is lighter. darken is the same, except the darker of the two pixels will be shown. The results of these are likely to be familiar to users of Photoshop or any other graphic-editing tool.

Examples	`li.shadowed {mix-blend-mode: darken;}`
	`aside {mix-blend-mode:`
	`    color-burn, luminosity, darken;}`

object-fit   Inh. N   Anim. N

Values	fill | contain | cover | scale-down | none
Initial value	fill
Computed value	As declared
Applies to	Replaced elements
Description	Alters the way an image's contents are sized with respect to its content box. The default, fill, causes the image to be stretched or squashed to fit its height and width, as images always have. none means the image keeps its intrinsic height and width, regardless of the values of the img element's height and width properties. contain will cause the entire image to be visible within its element box, scaled up or down as necessary, while maintaining its intrinsic aspect ratio. cover scales the image up or down to fill the image box of the image, again maintaining its intrinsic aspect ratio. scale-down means the image will stay its intrinsic size unless it's too big to fit into the element box, in which case it will be scaled down to fit.
Examples	img:nth-of-type(1) {object-fit: none;} img:nth-of-type(2) {object-fit: fill;} img:nth-of-type(3) {object-fit: cover;}

object-position   Inh. N   Anim. Y

Values	<position>
Initial value	50% 50%
Computed value	As declared
Applies to	Replaced elements
Description	Provides a way to change the position of a fitted image (see object-fit) within its element box, in a manner identical to how background origin images can be positioned.

| **Examples** | ```img:nth-of-type(1) {object-position: center;}```
```img:nth-of-type(2) {object-position: 67% 100%;}```
```img:nth-of-type(3) {object-position: left 142%;}``` |

opacity

Values	*<number>*
Initial value	1
Computed value	As declared
Applies to	All elements
Computed value	Same as declared (or a clipped value if declared value must be clipped)
Description	Defines an element's degree of opacity using a number in the range 0–1, inclusive. Any values outside that range are clipped to the nearest edge (0 or 1). This property affects every visible portion of an element. If it is necessary to have the content of an element semiopaque but not the background, or vice versa, use alpha color types such as rgba().

An element with opacity of 0 is effectively invisible and may not respond to mouse or other DOM events. Because of the way semiopaque elements are expected to be drawn, an element with opacity less than 1 creates its own stacking context even if it is not positioned. For similar reasons, an absolutely positioned element with opacity less than 1 and a z-index of auto force-alters the z-index value to 0. |
| **Examples** | ```h2 {opacity: 0.8;}```
```.hideme {opacity: 0;}``` |

order

Values	*<integer>*
Initial value	0
Computed value	As declared

Applies to	Flex and grid items, and the absolutely positioned children of flex and grid containers
Description	Sets a visual rendering order independently of the document source order. One example is turning a set of list items into flex items, and then designating a list item (or group of list items) from the middle of the list to be the first flex items displayed in the flex container. Because only the visual order is changed, not the DOM order, structural selectors like :first-child will match the first element in the source, not the first element on screen. Originally conceived as a way to change the visual layout order of flex items, this property now also allows authors to rearrange the order of auto-flowed grid items.
Examples	`li:nth-of-type(6) {order: 1;}` `li:nth-of-type(14) {order: -1;}`

orphans   Inh. N Anim. Y

Values	*<integer>*
Initial value	2
Computed value	As declared
Applies to	Block-level elements
Description	Defines the minimum number of text lines within an element that can be left at the bottom of a page. This can affect the placement of page breaks within the element.
Examples	`p {orphans: 4;}` `ul {orphans: 2;}`

outline   Inh. N Anim. P

Values	[*<outline-color>* ‖ *<outline-style>* ‖ *<outline-width>*]
Initial value	none
Computed value	As declared

Applies to	All elements
Animatable	Outline width and color; not style
Description	This is a shorthand property that defines the overall outline for an element. The most common use of outlines is to indicate which form element or hyperlink currently has focus (accepts keyboard input). Outlines can be of irregular shape, and no matter how thick, they do not change or otherwise affect the placement of elements.
Examples	`*[href]:focus {outline: 2px dashed invert;}` `form:focus {outline: outset cyan 0.25em;}`

outline-color   Inh. N Anim. Y

Values	*<color>*	invert
Initial value	invert
Computed value	As declared
Applies to	All elements
Description	Defines the color for the visible portions of the overall outline of an element. Remember that the value of outline-style must be something other than none for any visible border to appear. User agents are permitted to ignore invert on platforms that don't support color inversion. In that case, the outline's color defaults to the value of color for the element.
Examples	`*[href]:focus {outline-color: invert;}` `form:focus {outline-color: cyan;}`

outline-offset   Inh. N Anim. N

Values	*<length>*
Initial value	0
Computed value	An absolute length value
Applies to	All elements

Description	Defines the offset distance between the outer border edge and inner outline edge. Only one length value can be supplied, and it applies equally to all sides of the outline. Values can be negative, which causes the outline to "shrink" inward toward the element's center. Note that `outline-offset` cannot be set via the shorthand `outline`.
Examples	`*[href]:focus {outline-offset: 0.33em;}` `form:focus {outline-offset: -1px;}`

outline-style   Inh. N   Anim. N

Values	`auto` | `none` | `solid` | `dotted` | `dashed` | `double` | `groove` | `ridge` | `inset` | `outset`
Initial value	`none`
Computed value	As declared
Applies to	All elements
Description	Defines the style for the overall border of an element. The style must be something other than `none` for any outline to appear.
Examples	`*[href]:focus {outline-style: dashed;}` `form:focus {outline-style: outset;}`

outline-width   Inh. N   Anim. Y

Values	*<length>* | `thin` | `medium` | `thick`
Initial value	`medium`
Computed value	An absolute length, or 0 if the style of the outline is none; otherwise, as declared
Applies to	All elements
Description	Defines the width for the overall outline of an element. The width will take effect for a given outline only if the value of `outline-style` is something other than `none`. If the style *is* none, the width is

effectively reset to 0. Negative length values are not permitted.

Examples   `*[href]:focus {outline-width: 2px;}`
`form:focus {outline-width: 0.25em;}`

---

overflow   Inh. N   Anim. N

Values   `visible | hidden | scroll | auto`

Initial value   `visible`

Computed value As declared

Applies to   Block-level and replaced elements

Description   A shorthand property that defines what happens to content that overflows the content area of an element. For the value `scroll`, user agents should provide a scrolling mechanism whether or not it is actually needed; for example, scrollbars would appear even if all content can fit within the element box. If two values are supplied, the first defines the value of `overflow-x` and the second defines `overflow-y`. Otherwise, a single value defines both.

Examples   `#masthead {overflow: hidden;}`
`object {overflow: visible scroll;}`

---

overflow-wrap   Inh. Y   Anim. Y

Values   `normal | break-word`

Initial value   `normal`

Computed value As declared

Applies to   All elements

Description   Allows authors to specify whether line breaks are permitted inside words that are longer than their containing element is wide and which cannot be hyphenated, either due to language or the values of other properties. If `break-word` is set, the line-breaking will *only* occur if the word is placed on a new text line and still cannot fit inside its element's containing block. (This behavior is in contrast to word-break, which does not force a pre-word line break.)

Example   pre {overflow-wrap: break-word;}

Note   This property used to be called word-wrap. Browsers that supported word-wrap in the past now use it as an alias for overflow-wrap.

---

overflow-x   Inh. N   Anim. N

Values   visible | hidden | scroll | auto

Initial value   visible

Computed value   As declared

Applies to   Block-level and replaced elements

Description   Defines the overflow behavior along the horizontal (x) axis of the element; that is, the left and right edges of the element.

Examples   #masthead {overflow-x: hidden;}
object {overflow-x: visible;}

---

overflow-y   Inh. N   Anim. N

Values   visible | hidden | scroll | auto

Initial value   visible

Computed value   As declared

Applies to   Block-level and replaced elements

Description   Defines the overflow behavior along the vertical (y) axis of the element; that is, the top and bottom edges of the element.

Examples   #masthead {overflow-y: hidden;}
object {overflow-y: scroll;}

padding   Inh. N Anim. Y

Values	[<*length*> | <*percentage*>]{1,4}
Initial value	Not defined for shorthand elements
Computed value	See individual properties (`padding-top`, etc.)
Percentages	Refer to the width of the containing block
Applies to	All elements
Description	A shorthand property that defines the width of the overall padding for an element or sets the widths of each individual side's padding. Padding set on inline nonreplaced elements does not affect line-height calculations; therefore, such an element with both padding and a background may visibly extend into other lines and potentially overlap other content. The background of the element will extend throughout the padding. Negative padding values are not permitted.

Examples	`img {padding: 10px;}`
	`h1 {padding: 2ex 0.33em;}`
	`pre {padding: 0.75em 0.5em 1em 0.5em;}`

padding-bottom   Inh. N Anim. Y

Values	<*length*> | <*percentage*>
Initial value	0
Computed value	For percentage values, as declared; for length values, the absolute length
Percentages	Refer to the width of the containing block
Applies to	All elements
Description	Defines the width of the bottom padding for an element. Bottom padding set on inline nonreplaced elements does not affect line-height calculations; therefore, such an element with both bottom padding and a background may visibly extend into

other lines and potentially overlap other content. Negative padding values are not permitted.

Examples
```
ul {padding-bottom: 0.5in;}
h1 {padding-bottom: 2%;}
```

padding-left   Inh. N   Anim. Y

Values   *<length>* | *<percentage>*

Initial value   0

Computed value   For percentage values, as declared; for length values, the absolute length

Percentages   Refer to the width of the containing block

Applies to   All elements

Description   Defines the width of the left padding for an element. Left padding set for an inline nonreplaced element will appear only on the left edge of the first inline box generated by the element. Negative padding values are not permitted.

Examples
```
p {padding-left: 5%;}
pre {padding-left: 3em;}
```

padding-right   Inh. N   Anim. Y

Values   *<length>* | *<percentage>*

Initial value   0

Computed value   For percentage values, as declared; for length values, the absolute length

Percentages   Refer to the width of the containing block

Applies to   All elements

Description   Defines the width of the right padding for an element. Right padding set for an inline nonreplaced element will appear only on the right edge of the last inline box generated by the element. Negative padding values are not permitted.

Examples   img {padding-right: 30px;}
               ol {padding-right: 5em;}

padding-top   Inh. N Anim. Y

Values	*<length>*	*<percentage>*
Initial value	0
Computed value	For percentage values, as declared; for length values, the absolute length
Percentages	Refer to the width of the containing block
Applies to	All elements
Description	Defines the width of the top padding for an element. Top padding set on inline nonreplaced elements does not affect line-height calculations; therefore, such an element with both top padding and a background may visibly extend into other lines and potentially overlap other content. Negative padding values are not permitted.
Examples	ul {padding-top: 0.5in;} h3 {padding-top: 1.5em;}

page   Inh. N Anim. N

Values	*<identifier>*	auto
Initial value	auto
Computed value	As declared
Applies to	Block-level elements
Description	Defines the page type that *should* be used when displaying the element. The emphasis of the word "should" is taken directly from the specification, so author beware.
	The intended effect is that if an element has a value of page that is different than that of the preceding element, at least one page break is inserted before the element and a new page started using the page

type declared by page. (Multiple page breaks may be used if other styles call for using a right- or lefthand page when starting the new page.)

Examples
```
@page wide {size: landscape;}
table.summary {page: wide;}
```

page-break-after   Inh. N   Anim. N

Values	auto | always
Initial value	auto
Computed value	As declared
Applies to	Nonfloated block-level elements with a position value of relative or static
Description	Defines whether one or more page breaks should be placed after an element. Although it is theoretically possible to force breaks with always, it is not possible to guarantee prevention; avoid asks the user agent to avoid inserting a page break if possible. The keyword left is used to insert enough breaks after the element to make the next page be a lefthand page; similarly, right is used for a righthand page.
Examples	section {page-break-after: always;} h1 {page-break-after: avoid;}
Note	This property is essentially replaced by break-after, but browser support for page-break-after may be stronger.

page-break-before   Inh. N   Anim. N

Values	auto | always
Initial value	auto
Computed value	As declared
Applies to	Nonfloated block-level elements with a position value of relative or static

Description	Defines whether one or more page breaks should be placed before an element. It's theoretically possible to use always to force a page break, but while avoid asks the user agent to avoid inserting a page break if possible, there's no guarantee it won't insert one anyway. The keyword left is used to insert enough breaks before the element to make the page be a left-hand page; similarly, right is used for a righthand page.
Examples	`section {page-break-before: always;}` `h2 {page-break-before: avoid;}`
Note	This property is essentially replaced by break-before, but browser support for page-break-before may be stronger.

page-break-inside   Inh. Y Anim. N

Values	auto | avoid
Initial value	auto
Computed value	As declared
Applies to	Nonfloated block-level elements with a position value of relative or static
Description	Defines whether a page break should be avoided within the element. Note that such avoidance may not be possible; for example, declaring body {page-break-inside: avoid;} for a lengthy document will not prevent the insertion of page breaks by the user agent.
Example	`table {page-break-inside: avoid;}`
Note	This property is essentially replaced by break-before, but browser support for page-break-before may be stronger.

perspective   Inh. N Anim. Y

Values	none | <length>

Initial value	none
Computed value	The absolute length, or else none
Applies to	Any transformable element
Description	Defines the amount of apparent 3D perspective of an element's transformed children, but not for the element itself. Numbers define a foreshortening depth in pixels; smaller numbers define more extreme perspective effects. Negative values are treated the same as none.
Examples	``body {perspective: 250;} /* middlin' */`` ``#wrapper {perspective: 10;} /* extreme */``

perspective-origin   Inh. N Anim. P

Values	*<position>*
Initial value	50% 50%
Computed value	A percentage, except for length values, which are converted to an absolute length
Percentages	Refer to the size of the bounding box
Applies to	Any transformable element
Animatable	*<length>* and *<percentage>* values only
Description	Defines the origin point of the apparent 3D perspective within the element. In effect, it defines the point in the element that appears to be directly in front of the viewer.
Examples	``body {perspective-origin: bottom right;}`` ``#wrapper div {perspective-origin: 0 50%;}``

position   Inh. N Anim. N

Values	static | relative | sticky | absolute | fixed
Initial value	static
Computed value	As declared
Applies to	All elements

Description	Defines the positioning scheme used to lay out an element. Any element may be positioned, although an element positioned with absolute or fixed will generate a block-level box regardless of what kind of element it is. An element that is relatively positioned is offset from its default placement in the normal flow.
Examples	#footer {position: fixed; bottom: 0;} *.offset {position: relative; top: 0.5em;}

quotes
Inh. Y Anim. N

Values	[<string> <string>]+	none
Initial value	User agent–dependent
Computed value	As declared
Applies to	All elements
Description	Defines the quotation pattern used with quotes and nested quotes. The actual quote marks are inserted via the content property's open-quote and close-quote values.
Examples	q:lang(fr) {quotes: "«" "»" "‹" "›";} q {quotes: '\201C' '\201D' '\2018' '\2019';}

resize
Inh. N Anim. N

Values	none	both	horizontal	vertical
Initial value	none
Computed value	As declared
Applies to	Elements whose overflow value is not visible
Description	Defines how (or whether) an element can be resized by the user. The actual appearance and operation of any resize mechanism is left to the user agent and is likely dependent on the writing direction.
Examples	textarea {resize: vertical;} iframe {resize: both;}

right   Inh. N   Anim. P

Values	*<length>* | *<percentage>* | auto
Initial value	auto
Computed value	For static elements, auto; for length values, the corresponding absolute length; for percentage values, the specified value; otherwise, auto
Percentages	Refer to the height of the containing block
Applies to	Positioned elements
Animatable	*<length>* and *<percentage>* values only
Description	Defines the offset between the right outer margin edge of a positioned element and the right edge of its containing block.
Examples	`div#footer {position: fixed; right: 0;}` `*.overlapper {position: relative; right: -25px;}`

shape-image-threshold   Inh. N   Anim. Y

Values	*<number>*
Initial value	0.0
Computed value	The same as the specified value after clipping the *<number>* to the range [0.0, 1.0]
Applies to	Floats
Description	Changes the alpha channel value that acts as a threshold for float shape creation via an image. By default, only fully transparent areas in the shape's source image are used to define the float shape. If the value is changed to 0.7, then all areas of the source image that are 70% or more transparent are used to define the float shape. This allows for the same image to be used to define multiple float shapes, for example. A value of 0 will cause the entire image to be ignored for shape calculation.
Examples	`aside.illustrate {shape-image-threshold: 0.667;}` `img.floated {shape-image-threshold: 0.1;}`

shape-margin   Inh. N   Anim. Y

Values	*<length>* | *<percentage>*
Initial value	0
Computed value	An absolute length
Applies to	Floats
Description	Defines an offset distance between the edges of a float shape and the closest points at which text may approach the shape. This is useful when floating an image and using that same image to define the float shape, but wanting the keep normal-flow text away from the visible edges of the image. Note that the float shape and shape margin are clipped beyond the outer margin edge of the original float, so excessively large shape margins are most likely to result in a traditional rectangular float box.

Examples	`#one {shape-margin: 0;}`
	`#two {shape-margin: 1.5em;}`
	`#thr (shape-margin: 10%;}`

shape-outside   Inh. N   Anim. P

Values	none | [*<basic-shape>* ‖ *<shape-box>*] | *<image>*
Definitions	
<basic-shape>	`inset` | `circle()` | `ellipse()` | `polygon()`
<shape-box>	`margin-box` | `border-box` | `padding-box` | `content-box`
Initial value	none
Computed value	For a *<basic-shape>*, as defined for an *<image>*, its URI made absolute; otherwise, as declared
Applies to	Floats
Animatable	*<basic-shape>* values only
Description	Defines the shape of a floated element for the purposes of calculating text flow past the float. Possibilities include defining a polygon that echoes the outer

edge of an illustration, or using that image's transparent areas to define the float shape. Shapes are clipped at the edges of the shape's outer margin edge, so a float shape can never be larger than the unshaped version of that float.

Examples

```
img.web20 {shape-outside:
    inset(7% round 0.5em/5px);}
img.curio {shape-outside:
    circle(25px at 50% 50%);}
aside.diamond {shape-outside:
    polygon(50% 0, 100% 50%, 50% 100%, 0 50%);}
```

---

size   Inh. N   Anim. N

Values
auto | *<length>*{1,2} | [*<page-size>* || [portrait | landscape]]

Initial value
auto

Computed value
<length> values as absolute length values; otherwise, as declared

Applies to
The page area

Description
Defines the size and orientation of a page box. The keywords auto, portrait, and landscape cause the page box to fill the available rendering space on the page. Page boxes set to portrait have the content printed with the long sides of the page box being the right and left sides; in the case of landscape, the content is printed with the longer sides of the page box being the top and bottom sides.

If a page box is specified using lengths or one of the *<page-size>* keywords (e.g., A4) and the page box cannot be fit onto the actual page used for display, the page box and its contents may be scaled down to fit. If only one length value is declared, it sets both dimensions and thus defines a square page box. Length values that use em or ex units are calculated with respect to the computed font size of the page context.

Example
body {page-size: landscape;}

<page-size> is one of a defined set of standard page sizes; see Chapter 20 of *CSS: The Definitive Guide*, 4th Edition, for details.

tab-size   Inh. Y Anim. Y

Values	*<length>* | *<integer>*
Initial value	8
Computed value	The absolute-length equivalent of the value
Applies to	Block elements
Description	Sets the width of tab characters' whitespace when they are present in the displayed source *and* are honored for display due to the value of white-space. An *<integer>* value sets the number of "spaces" a tab character will generate.
Examples	`pre.source {tab-size: 4;}` `p.typer {tab-size: 0.25in;}`

table-layout   Inh. Y Anim. N

Values	auto | fixed
Initial value	auto
Computed value	As declared
Applies to	Elements with the display value table or inline-table
Description	Defines whether a table element should be laid out using an automatic-layout algorithm or a fixed-layout algorithm. The benefit of the automatic algorithm is that it's very similar to what authors are used to from more than a decade of browser behavior. However, the fixed-layout algorithm is theoretically faster and more predictable.
Examples	`table.data {table-display: fixed;}` `table.directory {table-display: auto;}`

text-align

Values	start | end | left | right | center | justify | match-parent | start end
Initial value	In CSS3, start; in CSS2.1, this was user agent–specific, likely depending on writing direction (e.g., left for Western languages like English)
Computed value	As declared, except in the case of match-parent
Applies to	Block-level elements
Description	Defines the horizontal alignment of text within a block-level element by defining the point to which line boxes are aligned. The value justify is supported by allowing user agents to programmatically adjust the word (but not letter) spacing of the line's content; results may vary by user agent.
Examples	p {text-align: justify;} h4 {text-align: center;}

text-align-last
Inh. Y   Anim. N

Values	auto | start | end | left | right | center | justify
Initial value	auto
Computed value	As declared
Applies to	Block-level elements
Description	Defines the horizontal alignment of the last line of text within a block-level element by defining the point to which line boxes are aligned. The value justify is supported by allowing user agents to programmatically adjust the word (but not letter) spacing of the line's content; results may vary by user agent.
Examples	p {text-align-last: justify;} h4 {text-align-last: right;}

text-decoration   Inh. N Anim. N

Values	none | [underline || overline || line-through || blink]
Initial value	none
Computed value	As declared
Applies to	All elements
Description	Defines text-decoration effects such as underlining. These decorations will span descendant elements that don't have decorations of their own, in many cases making the child elements appear to be decorated. Combinations of the values are legal. Any time two text-decoration declarations apply to the same element, the values of the two declarations are *not* combined. For example:

```
h1 {text-decoration: overline;}
h1, h2 {text-decoration: underline;}
```

Given these styles, h1 elements will be underlined with no overline because the value of underline completely overrides the value of overline. If h1 should have both overlines and underlines, use the value overline underline for the h1 rule and either move it after the h1, h2 rule or extend its selector to raise its specificity.

User agents are not required to support blink.

| **Examples** | ```
u {text-decoration: underline;}
.old {text-decoration: line-through;}
u.old {text-decoration: line-through underline;}
``` |

text-indent   Inh. Y Anim. Y

Values	*<length>* | *<percentage>*
Initial value	0
Computed value	For percentage values, as declared; for length values, the absolute length
```

Percentages	Refer to the width of the containing block
Applies to	Block-level elements
Description	Defines the indentation of the first line of content in a block-level element. This property is most often used to create a tab effect. Negative values are permitted and cause outdent (or hanging indent) effects. In CSS3, the value each-line will apply the indentation to any new line that results from a forced line break (e.g., due to a br element) within the element, not just the first line. The value hang ing inverts the defined pattern of indentation, allowing for the creation of an outdent effect without using a negative length value.
Examples	`p {text-indent: 5em;}` `h2 {text-indent: -25px;}`

text-orientation   Inh. Y Anim. Y

Values	mixed | upright | sideways
Initial value	mixed
Computed value	As declared
Applies to	All elements except table row groups, table rows, table column groups, and table columns
Description	Defines how characters are oriented in text, potentially independent of their writing mode (see writing-mode). When mixed, each character is aligned according to its language defaults as compared to the writing direction; for example, mixed English and Japanese text written in a vertical writing mode would have the English characters sideways and the Japanese characters upright. upright forces all characters to be upright regardless of their language, and sideways forces all characters to be shown sideways.

Examples	`#one {text-orientation: mixed;}`
	`#two {text-orientation: upright;}`
	`#thr {text-orientation: sideways;}`

text-rendering   Inh. Y Anim. Y

Values	auto	optimizeSpeed	optimizeLegibility	geometricPrecision
Initial value	auto
Computed value	As declared
Applies to	All elements
Description	Sets the approach used to render text, allowing authors to decide if speed, legibility, or precision is most important. Note that some user agents always optimize for legibility when rendering HTML text, so this property may have minimal or no effect outside of SVG (which is where it started out).
Examples	p {text-rendering: optimizeSpeed;} svg tspan {text-rendering: optimizeLegibility;}

text-shadow   Inh. N Anim. Y

Values	none	[<*length*> ‖ <*color*>? && <*length*>{2,3}]#
Initial value	none
Computed value	A color plus three absolute lengths
Applies to	All elements
Description	Defines one or more shadows to be "cast" by the text of an element. Shadows are always painted behind the element's text, but in front of the element's background, borders, and outline. Shadows are drawn from the first on top to the last on the bottom. The three length values that can be declared are, in order: horizontal offset, vertical offset, and blur distance. When positive, the offset values go down and to the right; when negative, they go back and to the left. Blur values cannot be negative.
Examples	h1 {text-shadow: 0.5em 0.33em 4px gray;} h2 {text-shadow: 0 –3px 0.5em blue;}

text-transform   Inh. Y Anim. N

Values	uppercase | lowercase | capitalize | none
Initial value	none
Computed value	As declared
Applies to	All elements
Description	Defines the pattern for changing the case of letters in an element, regardless of the case of the text in the document source. The determination of which letters are to be capitalized by the value `capitalize` is not precisely defined, as it depends on user agents knowing how to recognize a "word."
Examples	`h1 {text-transform: uppercase;}` `.title {text-transform: capitalize;}`

top   Inh. N Anim. P

Values	*<length>* | *<percentage>* | auto
Initial value	auto
Computed value	For static elements, auto; for length values, the corresponding absolute length; for percentage values, the specified value; otherwise, auto
Percentages	Refer to the height of the containing block
Applies to	Positioned elements
Animatable	*<length>* and *<percentage>* values only
Description	Defines the offset between the top outer margin edge of a positioned element and the top edge of its containing block.

Examples	`#masthead {position: fixed; top: 0;}`
	`sub {position: relative; top: 0.5em;`
	`    vertical-align: baseline;}`

Note	For relatively positioned elements, if both `top` and `bottom` are auto, their computed values are both 0. If one of them is auto, it becomes the negative of the

---

other; if neither is auto, bottom becomes the negative of the value of top.

transform   Inh. N Anim. P

Values	*<transform-list>* | none
Initial value	none
Computed value	As declared, except for relative length values, which are converted to an absolute length
Percentages	Refer to the size of the bounding box
Applies to	All elements except "atomic inline-level" boxes
Animatable	As a transform
Description	Defines one or more transforms of an element. These transforms can occur in a 2D or a simulated 3D space, depending on how the transforms are declared.
	The permitted values for *<transform-function>* are lengthy and complex. For a full list with minimalist descriptions, please consult the W3C's documentation on transform functions (*http://w3.org/TR/css3-3d-transforms/#transform-functions*).
Examples	`table th {transform: rotate(45deg);}` `li {transform: scale3d(1.2,1.7,0.85);}`

transform-origin   Inh. N Anim. P

Values	*<position>*
Initial value	50% 50%
Computed value	A percentage, except for length values, which are converted to an absolute length
Percentages	Refer to the size of the bounding box
Applies to	Any transformable element
Animatable	*<length>* and *<percentage>* values only

Description	Defines the origin point for an element's transforms in either 2D or simulated 3D space. The marked-as-optional *<length>* values are what define a 3D origin point; without them, the value is necessarily in 2D space.
| Examples | ```
table th {transform-origin: bottom left;}
li {transform-origin: 10% 10px 10em;}
``` |

transform-style   Inh. N Anim. N

Values	flat	preserve-3d
Initial value	flat
Computed value	As declared
Applies to	Any transformable element
Description	Defines whether an element transformed in simulated 3D space should have its children rendered using a flat style, thus putting them all in the same 2D plane as the element, or attempt to use a 3D effect where children with positive or negative z-index values may be rendered "in front of" or "behind" the element's plane as it rotates. Elements whose overflow value is hidden cannot preserve 3D effects and are treated as though the value of transform-style is flat.
Example	li {transform-style: preserve-3d;}

transition   Inh. N Anim. N

Values	[[none	*<transition-property>*] ‖ *<time>* ‖ *<transition-timing-function>* ‖ *<time>*]#
Initial value	all 0s ease 0s
Computed value	As declared
Applies to	All elements and :before and :after pseudo-elements
```

Description	A shorthand property that defines the aspects of one or more of an element's transitions from one state to another.
	Even though it is not (as of this writing) explicitly defined in the value syntax, descriptive text in the specification defines that when two *<time>* values are declared, the first is the duration and the second is the delay. If only one is declared, it defines only the duration.
Examples	`a:hover {transition: color 1s 0.25s ease-in-out;}` `h1 {transition: linear all 10s;}`

---

transition-delay Inh. N Anim. N

Values	*<time>*#
Initial value	0s
Computed value	As declared
Applies to	All elements and :before and :after pseudo-elements
Description	Defines a delay between when a transition could theoretically first start and when it actually starts. For example, if a transition is defined to begin on hover but has a delay of 0.5s, the transition will actually begin half a second after the element is first hovered over. Negative time values are permitted, but rather than creating a paradox, this simply jumps the transition to the point it would have reached had it been started at the defined time offset in the past. In other words, it will be started partway through the transition and run to its conclusion.
Examples	`a[href]:hover {transition-delay: 0.25;}` `h1 {transition-delay: 0;}`

---

transition-duration Inh. N Anim. N

Values	*<time>*#
Initial value	0s

Computed value	As declared
Applies to	All elements and :before and :after pseudo-elements
Description	Defines the length of time it takes for the transition to run from start to finish. The default 0s means the transition is instantaneous and no animation occurs. Negative time values are treated as 0s.
Examples	`a[href]:hover {transition-duration: 1s;}` `h1 {transition-duration: 10s;}`

transition-property   Inh. N Anim. N

Values	none | [all | <property-name>]#
Initial value	all
Computed value	As declared
Applies to	All elements and :before and :after pseudo-elements
Description	Defines one or more properties that are transitioned from one state to another; for example, color means that the foreground color of an element is transitioned from the start color to the finish color. If a shorthand property is declared, the transition parameters meant for that property are propagated to all the properties represented by the shorthand.

The keyword all means all properties are transitioned. The keyword none prevents any properties from being transitioned, effectively shutting down the transition. |
| **Examples** | `a[href]:hover {transition-property: color;}`
`h1 {transition-property: all;}` |

transition-timing-function   Inh. N Anim. N

Values	<timing-function>#

<timing-function> ease | linear | ease-in | ease-out | ease-in-out | cubic-bezier(*<number>*,*<number>*,*<number>*, *<number>*)

Initial value   ease

Computed value   As declared

Applies to   All elements and :before and :after pseudo-elements

Description   Defines the way in which intermediate states of a transition are calculated. The value keywords (ease, linear, etc.) are shorthands for specific cubic-bezier() values defined in the specification, so in effect all values of this property are cubic-bezier() values.

Examples
```
a[href]:hover {transition-timing-function:
   ease-in-out;}
h1 {transition-timing-function: linear;}
```

unicode-bidi   Inh. N Anim. Y

Values   normal | embed | bidi-override

Initial value   normal

Computed value   As declared

Applies to   All elements

Description   Allows the author to generate levels of embedding within the Unicode Bidirectional Algorithm. User agents that do not support bidirectional ("bidi") text are permitted to ignore this property.

Example
```
span.name {direction: rtl; unicode-bidi: embed;}
```

vertical-align   Inh. N Anim. P

Values   baseline | sub | super | top | text-top | middle | bottom | text-bottom | *<length>* | *<percentage>*

Initial value   baseline

Computed value	For percentage and length values, the absolute length; otherwise, as declared
Percentages	Refer to the value of line-height for the element
Applies to	Inline elements and table cells
Animatable	*\<length>* and *\<percentage>* values only
Description	Defines the vertical alignment of an inline element's baseline with respect to the baseline of the line in which it resides. Negative length and percentage values are permitted, and they lower the element instead of raising it. In table cells, this property sets the alignment of the content of the cell within the cell box. When applied to table cells, only the values baseline, top, middle, and bottom are recognized.
Examples	sup {vertical-align: super;} .fnote {vertical-align: 50%;}

visibility   Inh. Y Anim. N

Values	visible | hidden | collapse
Initial value	visible
Computed value	As declared
Applies to	All elements
Description	Defines whether the element box generated by an element is rendered. This means authors can have the element take up the space it would ordinarily take up, while remaining completely invisible. The value collapse is used in tables to remove columns or rows from the table's layout.
Examples	ul.submenu {visibility: hidden;} tr.hide {visibility: collapse;}

white-space   Inh. N Anim. N

Values	normal | nowrap | pre | pre-wrap | pre-line

Initial value	normal
Computed value	As declared
Applies to	All elements
Description	Defines how whitespace within an element is handled during layout. normal acts as web browsers have traditionally treated text, in that it reduces any sequence of whitespace to a single space. pre causes whitespace to be treated as in the HTML element pre, with both whitespace and line breaks fully preserved. nowrap prevents an element from line-breaking, like the nowrap attribute for td and th elements in HTML4. The values pre-wrap and pre-line were added in CSS2.1; the former causes the user agent to preserve whitespace while still automatically wrapping lines of text, and the latter honors newline characters within the text while collapsing all other whitespace as per normal.
Examples	td {white-space: nowrap;} tt {white-space: pre;}

widows   Inh. N Anim. Y

Values	*<integer>*
Initial value	2
Computed value	As declared
Applies to	Block-level elements
Description	Defines the minimum number of text lines within an element that can be left at the top of a page. This can affect the placement of page breaks within the element.
Examples	p {widows: 4;} ul {widows: 2;}

width   Inh. N Anim. Y

Values	*<length>*	*<percentage>*	auto

Initial value	auto
Computed value	For auto and percentage values, as declared; otherwise, an absolute length, unless the property does not apply to the element (then auto)
Percentages	Refer to the width of the containing block
Applies to	All elements except nonreplaced inline elements, table rows, and row groups
Description	Defines the width of an element's content area, outside of which padding, borders, and margins are added. This property is ignored for inline nonreplaced elements. Negative length and percentage values are not permitted.
| Examples | ```
table {width: 80%;}
#sidebar {width: 20%;}
.figure img {width: 200px;}
``` |

word-break   Inh. Y Anim. Y

Values	normal	break-all	keep-all
Initial value	normal
Computed value	As declared
Applies to	All elements
Description	Defines how text should be wrapped in situations where it would not ordinarily be wrapped; for example, a very long string of numbers containing no spaces, such as the first thousand digits of pi. The value break-all permits user agents to break a word (text string) at arbitrary points if it cannot find regular breakpoints within the word.
| Examples | ```
td {word-break: break-all;}
p {word-break: normal;}
``` |

word-spacing   Inh. Y Anim. Y

Values	<length>	normal

Initial value	normal
Computed value	For normal, the absolute length 0; otherwise, the absolute length
Applies to	All elements
Description	Defines the amount of whitespace to be inserted between words. Note that the specification does not define what constitutes a "word." In typical practice, user agents will apply this to the collapsed whitespace between strings of nonwhitespace characters. Negative length values are permitted and will cause words to bunch closer together.

Examples	`p.spacious {word-spacing: 6px;}`
	`em {word-spacing: 0.2em;}`
	`p.cramped {word-spacing: -0.5em;}`

writing-mode   Inh. Y Anim. Y

Values	horizontal-tb | vertical-rl | vertical-lr
Initial value	horizontal-tb
Computed value	As declared
Applies to	All elements except table row groups, table column groups, table rows, table columns, Ruby base containers, and Ruby annotation containers
Description	Allows the author to change the writing method used to flow text and other inline content into the element. The vertical values are useful for languages that are primarily vertical, as is the case with many non-Roman languages. It is possible to have text from a normally horizontal language (e.g., German or Hebrew) flowed into a vertical writing mode, though the orientation of the characters may not be as expected (see `text-orientation`). Similarly, it's possible to take a normally vertical language and flow it horizontally with `horizontal-tb`.
Examples	`[lang="en"] {writing-mode: horizontal-tb;}` `[lang="jp"] {writing-mode: vertical-rl;}`

z-index   Inh. N   Anim. Y

Values	*\<integer>* | auto
Initial value	auto
Computed value	As declared
Applies to	Positioned elements
Description	Defines the placement of a positioned element along the z-axis, which is defined to be the axis that extends perpendicular to the display area. Positive numbers are closer to the user, and negative numbers are farther away.
Example	`#masthead {position: relative; z-index: 10000;}`

Index

About the Author

Eric A. Meyer has been working with the web since late 1993 and is an internationally recognized expert on the subjects of HTML, CSS, and web standards. A widely read author, he is CTO at Rebecca's Gift (*http://rebeccasgift.org/*), a 501(c)(3) nonprofit organization dedicated to providing healing family vacations after the death of a child; and is, along with Jeffrey Zeldman (*http://www.zeldman.com/*), cofounder of An Event Apart (*https://aneventapart.com/*).

Beginning in early 1994, Eric was the visual designer and campus web coordinator for the Case Western Reserve University website (*https://case.edu/*), where he authored a widely acclaimed series of HTML tutorials and was project coordinator for the online version of the *Encyclopedia of Cleveland History* (*http://case.edu/ech/*) combined with the *Dictionary of Cleveland Biography*, the first example of an encyclopedia of urban history being fully and freely published on the web. He has written several books on CSS and design, and shares what he has learned at conferences the world over and at his personal site *meyerweb.com*. In 2006, he was inducted into the International Academy of Digital Arts and Sciences (*https://www.iadas.net/*) for "international recognition on the topics of HTML and CSS" and helping to "inform excellence and efficiency on the Web."

Eric lives with his family in Cleveland, Ohio, which is a much nicer city than you've heard. He enjoys a good meal whenever he can and considers almost every form of music to be worthwhile.

Learn from experts.
Find the answers you need.

Sign up for a **10-day free trial** to get **unlimited access** to all of the content on Safari, including Learning Paths, interactive tutorials, and curated playlists that draw from thousands of ebooks and training videos on a wide range of topics, including data, design, DevOps, management, business—and much more.

Start your free trial at:
oreilly.com/safari

(No credit card required.)